My Encounters with the Spirit World

J. B. Duncan

BALBOA.
PRESS

A DIVISION OF HAY HOUSE

Edited by C. Duncan
A.C.E. Editing Services
P.O. Box 484 Taree 2430
N.S.W. Australia
kirin@midcoast.com.au

Interior Graphics/Art Credit: Christine Duncan

Balboa Press books may be ordered through booksellers or by contacting:

Balboa Press
A Division of Hay House
1663 Liberty Drive
Bloomington, IN 47403
www.balboapress.com.au
1-(877) 407-4847

ISBN: 978-1-4525-0448-3 (sc)
ISBN: 978-1-4525-0449-0 (e)

Printed in the United States of America

Balboa Press rev. date: 07/27/2012

This book is dedicated to my husband, Clive,
for your endless love and patience, I love you.

To my youngest daughter, Christine,
who helped me with editing.

And to my late father, and late son, Arthur,
also my lady in spirit who inspired and guided me.

And to all of those in the spirit world
who have helped me create this book

୫୦୧୫

Table of Contents

PART ONE: MY EARLY YEARS

PART TWO: THE CHANGE OF A LIFETIME

List of Pictures

PART ONE

MY EARLY YEARS

Chapter One

DISCOVERY

The Doll in the Wardrobe and God

What would you do if you saw a ghost for the very first time? Would you scream? Run away? Most likely you would do what I did – freeze. Only, my first ghost was a bit more than that . . .

My story begins when I was ten years old. Mum and Dad, with my two sisters and my brother, migrated to Australia from England and arrived here on the 12th February 1951 – my younger sister's third birthday. My other sister and brother are twins and three years older than me. We settled in a small but comfy three-bedroom house in a small country town called Warragamba Dam of N.S.W.

Soon after settling into our new home I started lessons at my first Australian school. I was reasonably happy there most of the time but hated going when my English-born teacher was there. Tall and arrogant, he reprimanded me very angrily whenever I failed to apply 'proper' pronunciations. I spoke in my native broad Geordies accent and he insisted I speak Australian right away.

"It's not Goood-dair," he would say. "You're in Australia now! It's Good-dye!"

I turned eleven the following August and this is when the spiritual encounters started. It was about four weeks before Christmas and my younger sister was in a mood for misbehaving. She was a typical three year old, wanting attention, when Mum said, "If you are a good girl, Santa will bring you a beautiful black doll with pretty long plaits."

My sister burst into tears.

"I don't want a black doll! I don't like black dolls!" she cried.

Mum frowned, clearly very distressed. "Now what will I do? I've spent a lot of money on it and can't take it back now," she muttered and walked away.

I followed her, wanting to let her know I would quite happily take it instead.

"Don't worry, Mum," I quietly said. "I'll have it, if that's o.k. with you."

A big smile appeared on her face and she gave me a hug.

"Thank you, dear," she replied, "that is a big relief."

About two weeks before Christmas I grew curious, wondering what the doll looked like. I couldn't find it no matter where I looked.

"Where did you hide the doll, Mum?" I casually asked her as she passed by one day.

She replied automatically. "It's on the top shelf in my wardrobe. Why?"

"Oh, no reason, just curious," I muttered and quietly went on reading my school book, hoping she couldn't read my mind.

Around eight o'clock a night or two later I could hold back no more, choosing that part of the evening when the family was distracted with listening to the radio, our humble entertainment before television appeared. What followed was very humbling indeed and was an experience I've never forgotten since.

The wardrobe was in the corner immediately on my left-hand side, (as you walked through the door, facing Mum's bed). Opposite the bedroom door and wardrobe was a long, four-paned window fronting the street, where a streetlight was on, providing just enough light in the darkness.

A mirror was mounted down the middle of the two doors of the wardrobe, which reflected the opposite corner of the room and captured half of the very large window in its reflection, too. Some ten to twelve feet, (3-4 meters) separated this corner of the house from the ground outside, in which another room could've been built beneath, however it had been left empty, with only vertical stilts exposed.

After checking to see that no one was watching me – nor could see me – I cheekily approached the wardrobe and, in the darkened interior, quietly opened the door. Without a backward glance I reached up to the top shelf, intending to get the doll down, unwrap it and discover just how pretty she was. Then I became aware of an unusually bright light shining into the mirror, where, as I now stared, a god-like figure had appeared. I froze on the spot.

Clothed in gold-embroidered white robes, golden cord round His waist and wearing a crown, I thought I was staring at God Himself. Then I thought, *it must be Jesus*, because this was the image taught to us in Sunday

3

school. No matter what, it was incredible to see and it still put the fear of Him in me anyway!

Then suddenly thinking it was a reflection from the corner window, I quickly looked behind me, certain he'd have to be standing behind me but outside the window there. Sure enough, the unhappy face of Jesus was looking back at me, with his head slowly moving from side to side in a very disappointed way and with a raised index finger waving reproachfully. Clearly he was saying, "That's not right".

I was caught in the act and by the Almighty Himself! What a naughty girl I was!

The sickly feeling of having been 'sprung' made me hurry up and close the wardrobe door, but on turning to the mirror I found the reflection of Jesus was gone. I immediately looked to the window again – yet he was still there! This time I noticed he seemed to be hovering in the air, although his expression hadn't changed.

I stopped what I was doing and raced outside, (through the lounge room, between the sofa and radio that the family members were listening to), I went down the steps towards the driveway to see if anyone was playing a trick on me. But no, there was nothing to indicate anyone had ever been there – with, or without, a ladder. Now very confused, I went back inside and cautiously returned to Mum's bedroom, opened the door and peered over to the corner window, though not game enough to go right in. True to form He was there and this time, smiling gently.

I took this as my cue to leave well enough alone. I felt I had been warned and saved from receiving a terrible punishment off my mother, whose temper was short and often quite severe. She'd have undoubtedly been furious if I had seen the doll before Christmas and at eleven years old, I was impatient.

Yet the experience of having to wait was rewarding and when I was finally given the present – which couldn't be opened quickly enough – I suspect my face must have said it all, because Mum seemed more excited than I to learn that I adored the doll. She was beautiful and sixty years later I still have her, a little battered, yet in tact. The wardrobe with the mirror down the middle is also with me!

From the start I had felt this 'other person' had wanted me to have her, a spiritual someone, so I assumed a special responsibility for her and in my late teens, a child had been playing roughly with her, ruining her hair and virtually causing her wig to fall off. Promptly I took her to a doll's hospital in Sydney, where after a face-lift and make-over, I brought her home again. She wasn't quite the same as before, but I wanted her back because I loved her.

I know I'll never forget what I saw in the mirror that night and to this day, I feel like I saw God. If it wasn't Him, then it may have been Jesus, or some beautiful biblical person or maybe it was only an angel. Whoever it was, He was warning me, "Don't you look at that doll!" – because it would've spoilt the surprise.

As time went on, I suspected only a few people ever believed me when I spoke of this encounter. There were those who'd said I had been deceived by the devil. These days I can understand these comments as coming from those who either fear the unknown, or try to analyse it. They might also be too lodged in a religious 'block'.

A few people did listen and didn't argue against these thoughts, yet most sneered at me on hearing this story, so I eventually stopped telling it, until now. In fact, it is here in my current stage of life that I have been prompted by Spirit; I must tell of all of my encounters in a book *if I am to regain the full gifts of psychic awareness,* which I had regrettably given away in the early eighties.

This, too, will unfold in the pages to come, yet for the present, I am driven by Spirit's need for me to get this message across: never deny yourself, or Spirit, the gifts of communicating with Spirit, or those in the spiritual realms. For once you send it away, like I had, it may never be given back to you and it is a very special blessing to have. Great healing can come to those who are grieving in the absence of a departed loved one. Significant wisdom can be given to those who listen. And immense relief can come to those who have passed who did not get the opportunity to say good bye. Everyone is affected, in many ways and on many levels. Sometimes even spirits need 'rescuing', because occasionally they may not have realised their earth bodies have died and are thus left in a 'limbo like' state of being.

And to those of you who are new to psychic experiences, such as seeing or hearing 'ghosts', never, ever, feel afraid. First and foremost, you are being looked after, guided by and guarded by higher beings who love you. *They* won't let harm be done to you, nor can a 'ghost' hurt you (contrary to the impression that many television shows and movies inspire!). You will also find any family members or friends you have known that have passed over will have likely taken up a protective role over you, or at least will choose to stay close by you. If at any time you feel threatened or fearful, ask them or your God for protection and imagine you are in a bubble. Learn to accept their presence, feel their love and welcome their help or advice.

In time your abilities will strengthen and grow.

You must learn it [the gift(s)], to earn it.

⁎⁎⁎

Although I was once a sceptic, I also kept an open mind to everything. It used to irritate me when I heard people saying of psychic things, "That's nonsense, there's nothing after we've gone. When you're dead, you're dead." But what really got to me was, "There's no such things as ghosts or spirits" (that used to really rile me). Even though at the time I had not seen any such beings – apart from Jesus in the wardrobe mirror – I couldn't dismiss it. Others would say, "You have to be born with it", but then those same others still didn't believe the people who could 'do it' even when they'd said they *had* spoken to spirit people!

Psychics and mediums were thought of as "nuts" or whackos, so I was told. They were, "People who should be locked up", or who had "just got out of the loony bin", because they were supposedly hallucinating. This is what I was led to believe of them, though I never really discarded the thought there might have been some truth in it all. Nevertheless, I was terrified if I ever was to see anything or anyone, say something and be put away for a long time, so I remained reserved. However, like I said, I kept an open mind.

⁎⁎⁎

The wardrobe in which my doll was hidden

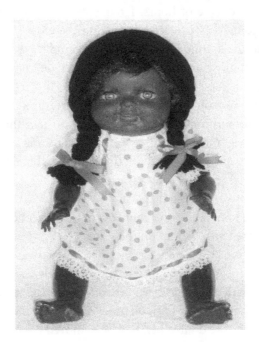

The black doll Mum gave me for Christmas

The Glass Crystal Ball

A year later we moved from this house. In fact, we had three moves within five years and in my late teens, I was reintroduced to the Spirit World. Mum took to inviting mediums to our 'new' home (approximately every three to four months apart). At first I thought she was simply inviting people for afternoon tea, which was not an unusual affair at the time, only, the strangest of them to me, at least, was our first medium, Mrs. Glass.

I describe her build as 'butch', or like a short, army major. However she proved to be a very nice lady, although her arrival was rather odd indeed.

"She's here," Mum called and opened the front door to greet her. She then took her straight down the hall to our second bedroom.

I thought she must have felt tired or sick or something, for she stayed there for up to a couple of hours. I remember watching Mum's 'guests' take turns in going down to see her, staying there for a little while, then coming back to the lounge room as another would leave for the bedroom, each one commenting on how 'good' she was on their return. It was extraordinary.

Their chatter went on to discuss things of sadness as well as of excitement to come, or of something that had happened to them that this lady had picked up on. I began to think they were playing some sort of mysterious game, right up until the last person left for the day. Finally Mum went in and when she emerged, she, too, was excited.

"What's going on?" I asked at last.

"She told me I am going on a long journey," she replied. "And possibly two of my children will end up on the stage."

She was obviously pleased for she then invited my older sister and brother and me, into the room to see the 'good' lady.

In there a small table had been set in front of the window, with just enough room for one person to sit on one side of it and this 'butch' woman to sit on the other. The double bed had been moved hard against the wall.

A pretty cloth covered the table and on it was placed a crystal ball. Gently we were ushered nearer to it.

"Mrs. Glass," Mum said to her, "the kids are interested in what you are doing. Could you show them please?"

You could've knocked me down with a feather; Mrs. Glass . . . with a glass ball! This one took the cake! But as I looked into that glass ball while the lady described what she could see, I, too, began to see something the closer I stared and it was not due to a child's active imagination. I saw a steam train travelling along a mountain track quite clearly (steam trains were our only rail transport then). To me, it could've meant anything – quite simply, it was a train. Was it really to be taken as a literal journey? Where was Mum supposed to be going?

It wasn't until years later I realised the lady was using what is called the 'Third Eye' and not the actual ball. She was feeling the energies with her hands, which were only holding the ball. It was weird to me that the others couldn't see anything but a crystal surface, though I have since suspected this lady must have realised I had 'the Gift', too, although apparently had said nothing of it to my mother.

I don't know what the train journey might have meant for Mum, (or even if the train appeared in Mum's reading; she never gave details of her messages). On reflection, however, I feel that *my* moving steam train signified my own spiritual journey, one which would take me over emotional hurdles (the mountains) with the smoke puffs representing 'ghosts', or spirits. Needless to say, both my older sister and brother have – respectively – performed on stage over the years, my sister with acting and my brother with singing.

ॐ☙☞

The Premonition Gift

I married Clive in 1961, we bought a house in the hills district of Sydney, NSW and around 1965, with two infants to raise and a third baby on the way, the gift of premonition came to me, even though I wasn't aware of it at first. I guess things like this tend to sneak up on us.

One day, as I was sitting outside on the back steps looking out over the backyard, I tried to think of the words to write in my letter to a magazine. An article about premonitory experiences and abilities which asked the readers to send in details of anyone who'd had any premonitions for the firm, Hay House, in London, England.

Though I'd never before considered I possessed such gifts, I began to write about the small things I had experienced that year. Things do not happen by chance and when 'something funny' occurs, I often see it as being a sign from Spirit.

Just then, an aeroplane flew overhead.

I wrote:

> *"Sometimes I can predict small aircraft about to crash and sometimes I can predict an accident that has happened ahead when travelling in the car with friends or relatives and as I'm writing this to you now, a large plane is flying over my house some thirty thousand feet up in the air. It appears to be making a funny noise just like the ones I've heard in the smaller planes, so I guess by the time you get this a crash may have already happened. I also feel I can see flames coming from it and while it is landing at a big airport, I can see people jumping off the left wing. There is a rock star jumping from the wing, he doesn't appear to be very badly hurt but there is a lot of passengers who are badly bruised and bleeding."*

Within the week I heard on the evening news that a large plane had landed miraculously at Heathrow airport in England, on fire and with most of its passengers seen jumping off the left wing. The media also reported, ". . . rock star, Marcus Holden*, has had a lucky escape. He survived by jumping off the tip of the wing, leaving him in shock and badly bruised. He was taken to hospital and last we heard is that he will be okay. Now on with the local news . . ." [* unfortunately I cannot remember his surname with accuracy all of these years later, but I do think this is a close approximation.]

This left me quite shaken and all week I was wondering what was going to happen next. I felt there was more to come. Sure enough, a month and a half later as I was going to bed and after saying "goodnight" to my husband I turned off the bed lamp. By the small glow from the street light outside of our front room I snuggled into my pillow, when all of a sudden I heard screaming voices around me.

Thinking someone had broken in, I jumped out of bed and I turned on the light.

"Are you okay?" my husband asked.

"I heard people screaming and thought someone had broken in," I replied, but of course there was no one around. Then I thought it must have been hooligans running up or down our street, so we turned the light off so they wouldn't see us through the window. In the quiet that followed I nervously tried to settle down again.

A couple of minutes later not only did I hear people crying but I also felt I was being watched. I opened my eyes into the darkened room and in the glow from the street light I saw, to my horror, all these sad eyes everywhere, all around me, even on top of my wardrobe. It was very scary.

I looked to my husband's side of the bed and in the dim-lit corner beyond, I saw the face of the then president of America, Lynden B. Johnson. I was terrified, not knowing what it all meant. I threw on the light again and watched all the eyes and the face of Mr. Johnson fade slightly but not completely; they were sort of transparent and all very sad.

Clive woke up to find me shaking, not knowing what to do. He was clearly worried and asked what he could do to help me settle.

"If you don't mind, could I possibly leave the little light on all night, because I think this would help me a lot?" I said, feeling that 'they' wouldn't attack me if light surrounded me. He agreed and cuddled up to me and after a while I must have dozed off.

The next morning we turned the radio on, only to hear of the dreadful event which had taken place in America hours earlier for, while we were trying to sleep here in Australia, it was daytime there. Martin Luther King had been assassinated; the people were wild with emotion. President Lynden B. Johnson had sent his condolences to all the black people and expressed his sadness, saying that he would attend his funeral.

We were horrified and slowly I realised I must have been there when it had happened, (astral travelled), or that he was trying to reach out to me. Though the news was so shocking, it was also a big relief for me, for I could understand now what my experience during the night had been – a clear psychic link to a world event thousands of miles away.

As my premonitions got stronger each day I learned not to be scared of them, but to try to understand how it connected to what was happening around me, to work with it than to be frightened of it.

⋙⋘

Chapter Two

A FATHER'S LOVE

Kissed By A Spirit

In December 1968 my father took very ill and had to go to hospital. I was four weeks pregnant with my fourth child when we went to visit him, though no one else knew except for my husband. Christmas was always an occasion in which my Dad loved to put up the Christmas lights and streamers and, because he was bound to a hospital bed, he was therefore unable to join in with decorating the house. He grew anxious, showing signs of stress, which possibly added to the decline in his health.

This, of course, had affected Mum, so the family had rallied around and helped to put up the streamers. Although Dad seemed happier when we told him, you could see he was upset for he wished to go home. It was not quite two weeks after the New Year when medical tests showed he wasn't improving, that in fact, his condition was now likely to be terminal.

Feeding tubes had been inserted in his nose and down the back of his throat, constricting his vocal chords and interfering with his ability to communicate. Understandably Mum was upset because he couldn't talk to her. She hoped he would somehow respond to her, but depressed with the results, she decided to go home with my older sister and her family for lunch.

For me it was a chance to try something on him I'd seen in a television movie and, it also turned out to be another important learning curve. Some ten minutes passed in which I talked with Dad as best I could and like with Mum and the others, the conversation was one-sided. Knowing how hard it must have been for him to answer, I remembered a particular scene from a black and white film and decided to give it a go.

"Dad," I said, "I would like to try something. I know you can hear me, so blink once for 'yes' and twice for 'no'." I then asked, "Are you comfortable?"

He slowly blinked once.

I asked him a 'no' question and he struggled with two blinks, while his eyes filled with tears.

It made me sad to watch how those tears ran down the side of his face. Reaching for a tissue to dry them, I told him how glad I was that we seemed to have worked this out and went on to share a small but excited conversation with him, in which I still hadn't told him about the expected baby.

Mum returned two hours later.

Dad was now smiling a little and I could sense he wanted me to tell her of our breakthrough.

"I have something good to tell you," I said to her as she bent over Dad to give him a kiss on the cheek. She stood up to listen.

"We can communicate with Dad for you!" *

She reared up almost in anger.

"How can you when he can't talk properly!? Don't be silly!"

I looked down at Dad. His face had turned unhappy again.

"Look, I'll show you. If you ask him a 'yes' question, he'll blink once and a 'no' question, he'll blink twice. Watch." So I asked Dad if he'd blink once to show Mum how we had worked it out.

He did, very slowly, but he'd managed it.

Mum looked at him and said, "How do you know he wasn't blinking only normally?"

So I asked him a 'no' question.

He struggled on, blinking twice.

Mum bristled even more.

"That's no proof!" she stated vigorously. "He might be just normally blinking!"

With this, tears rolled down my father's now very sad face. I can still vividly see it today – I wanted to cry for him, I believed I knew exactly how he was feeling.

I felt Dad saying to me, *'Don't worry, she doesn't want to understand. So don't even try it again, okay?'*

---

* (As I narrate this story to my daughter – the expected baby of this story – who is helping me to type these words into a legible format, I hear my father say, in reference to the eyes blinking "Huh, that was a bloody mistake, wasn't it?" A moment on and my mother – also in spirit – followed by saying, "Well I didn't bloody know, did I?")

So I said to him, in front of Mum, "Don't worry, we understand. We'll just talk to you between ourselves," and I wiped his tears away and continued to talk to him as usual, until Mum realised I wasn't joking. I felt that after about half an hour of this, she saw what was happening and was sort of wanting to believe what she was seeing.

On leaving Dad around dinner time, I finished off saying, "Love you Dad, see you tomorrow. Hope you'll feel better then."

His eyes filled with water; I detected a smile of "thank you".

"Goodnight," I whispered, while firmly holding his hand. I didn't realise this would be for the last time.

The next morning around nine a.m. my husband, my sister, her two children and my three children, along with Mum, piled into our small Hillman car – in those days we didn't have seat belts and were allowed to nurse children on our knees.

We headed off to Sydney, thirty minutes drive away from home, for important family business matters including a ten o'clock appointment for Mum, after which we planned to visit Dad in the hospital again.

Some ten minutes after leaving the city, around two p.m. we were stopped at an intersection in Balmain. Ryde Hospital, where my father waited, was still about thirty minutes away. Unfortunately it was now very close for peak-hour traffic on the roads and the delay was noticeable. All of a sudden I felt this cold kiss on my right cheek. I looked at my husband – our driver and therefore seated on my right – who was now touching his left cheek.

"Did you feel that?" I whispered quietly to him, hoping the passengers in the back seat wouldn't hear us.

He went pale. "Yes," he answered.

Instinctively we both felt it was my father behind it.

"Dad, quick!" we said simultaneously.

With this he put his foot down as the lights turned green and sped through the traffic as fast as he could safely go. When we reached the hospital, Mum, my sister and my husband, left me to look after the kids while they went in to check on Dad. I was so hurt, as I wanted to go too, after all, it *was* my Dad, not my husband's.

After about ten minutes of trying to keep the kids amused in the car, a smallish young nurse appeared from the building and walked towards me. When she was close enough, she broke the bad news that I didn't want to hear. She told me to go on up to be with the others as she was going to keep an eye on the kids.

When I reached my family, they were gathered in the hall outside the reception area, they said he had died about twenty minutes earlier; this was when my husband and I had felt the icy cold kiss on our cheeks. I now know it was Dad's way of saying goodbye to us and I went to his bedside and returned his kiss on his forehead.

I was sad that I'd never got to tell my father I was expecting again, but something inside me told me he already knew.

››‹‹

Dad's Smile

I received a visit from my father two months after he'd passed. It had been a very tiring day with the demands of the two younger children and now that they had settled on their beds and fallen asleep, I too, decided to take a nap. This was around two in the afternoon, just before my eldest son was due to come out of kindergarten.

I happened to be facing my wardrobe when I lay down. It was Mum and Dad's maple wood bedroom suite which they gave me when we bought our new home. Mum gave it to us because we couldn't afford much furniture. I hadn't been thinking of anything in particular other than the need for rest before picking up my son by three p.m. Within a few minutes I was comfortable and dozing pleasantly, when suddenly I was startled wide awake. Dad's face had appeared on the wardrobe's polished door!

At first I thought I was imagining things, but each time I looked away and then back again, I saw his image. He was smiling brilliantly. It was as though he was thinking, *'At last she can see me!'*

A surge of relief came over me. I felt calm and relaxed and mentally sent him my thoughts.

'If I can really see you, let me have a little girl,' I said. *'For if I have a boy, I will have to rearrange the bedrooms to accommodate three boys.'* I could only hope he was hearing me. *'This way,'* I went on, (a touch sceptically, I might add), *'if I have a girl, they can stay in the same rooms, with two boys in one and two girls in the other. If it's God's will, please help me to have a girl and then I'll believe in the Spirit World.'*

I was blessed with seeing Dad on numerous occasions while pregnant with this baby. There was an 'eerie' experience when both my husband and I saw him on the side of a moving car. One day while we were cleaning up in our bedroom, we heard a strange noise coming from outside, almost as if there was a lot of people shouting and screaming. We just looked at each other and I blurted out, "Dad's coming!"

We raced out to the front door and looked down the street to the T-junction two houses away, when we saw a car of the same make and model to what Dad had had; same shape, slightly different colour. On the driver's door we saw the same face I had seen on the wardrobe only weeks before; it was a huge smile (only a larger face here). It was brilliant, because my husband confirmed that he saw it too. We can't explain the noise of shouting and screaming as there was only the driver in it, but we felt it was Dad's way of getting us outside to see him, just to let us know he was still around.

In the August of 1969 our baby was born; a girl, who not only looked like Dad, but, uncannily, had also adopted his habit of putting the tongue to the corner of the mouth just between the lips, exactly like Dad did when working on his car, or with items in his garage. Even when she'd spat out her dummy, her tongue poked out the corner of her mouth! As she grew older the habit persisted when she played with her toys, especially when she was deep in thought or concentrating with things, but eventually the tendency stopped during her early school days. It always made me feel as though Dad was with her, or perhaps reincarnated in her, (however in her adult years she took on her own personality traits). It was interesting to note that, up until her mid twenties, she had commented on having often felt his presence around her.

ՑՕՇՑ

My Dad, David Duncan, approximate age, 51

Baby Visions for my Doctor

After about six months of being pregnant with my fourth child I started to get premonitions of things that were about to happen to people I knew – and some I had never met. I remember one time when I was visiting our local doctor for my check up, where I had had a vision of him holding a baby that morning in a house. Then just as I was getting up from the chair to leave, I had this urge to look at him and say, "Is your wife pregnant?"

I had never met his wife so I didn't know how he would react. The doctor sat straight up in his chair.

"Why, who told you?" he said.

"No one," I answered. "Do any of the doctors in the surgery have a rectangle-shaped lounge room with green coloured walls?" I also described where each piece of furniture was positioned.

He went pale. I thought he may have wondered if I had been spying on him.

"Yes, I have," he replied with a worried look on his face. "But how do you know all that?"

"I had a vision of you holding a little baby on your left arm," I said, "while your wife, who is a bit shorter than you, is standing beside you, with her left arm around the front of the baby and her right arm around your waist. It's as though I was looking at a baby's card with the words, 'It's a boy!' written above your heads."

He was stunned.

"Thanks," he said shakily. "We'll see what happens in a couple of months."

After my daughter Christine's birth, I visited him again for my monthly check ups.

"You were right," he said with a big grin on his face. "My wife gave birth to a son last week and all went well. Thank you."

Of course, I was very happy for them. About two years later I took Christine for a check up to the same doctor when I had another premonition that morning. Again, just as I was about to leave the surgery I brazenly asked if his wife was expecting another baby. He seemed shocked at what I had just said.

"Yes, but how did you know?" he said. "I haven't told anyone yet as I have only just found out about five minutes before you came in. My wife just rang and told me the good news after she went for her check up this morning."

I went on to tell him of my vision. "Before leaving home this morning I got this vision just like before, only you were holding the older one on your left arm and your wife was holding the new baby boy on her right arm. So both boys were in the middle of you two, with the name 'Boy! Boy! Boy!' spread all over the card."

"Okay," he said, "we'll see in nine month's time if you are right."

I smiled cheekily at him as I walked out of the room, but as he was closing the door I noticed a look of bewilderment on his face.

About ten months later I took all four of my children to the doctor for their booster needles. As we walked into his room he started grinning from ear to ear.

"I don't know how you did it again; twice," he began, "but we had another boy three weeks ago. You're amazing!"

I felt good, for I knew now that I was getting much stronger.

Approximately eighteen months had gone by when I had to visit him for a minor ailment. When he opened the door of his surgery and saw me, I could see the worried lines on his face, as if he were secretly wondering what I might say. After the consultation and as I was preparing to leave, I asked the same question as before.

"Is your wife off again?"

"Okay, yes," he said. "She is three months. And what do you think she's having this time?"

"Well, I'm confused," I answered, "because I think you would like a little girl, but I feel it's another boy. When it is born it could be a girl that has the look of a boy, or it'll be a boy with a cute girlish face."

"Well I don't mind either way," he responded, "as long as it's healthy."

"As much as I hope it's a girl for you," I said, "I have no letters or names to indicate what it'll be, but the face I saw in my vision looked like a little girl. But inwardly I felt it was another boy."

He said there was nothing we could do about it; whatever will be will be and as it turned out, I was right again. They had a third son whose face looked like a pretty little girl (so I was told). To this day I have never met Dr. Tony's wife or his children, though it would have been nice to see them in person or in a photo, for conformation of my visions.

એ૦જી

The Winning Barbecue Cake

The countless times I dreamed of my father was enormous. I remember – vividly – one dream that came ten years after Christine's birth. It's one I'll never forget, one that I'll take to the grave with me and when I see my father again, he'll get the biggest hug I can give him. You see, I was in the habit of making and decorating cakes for the annual Castle Hill agriculture shows, but this year I couldn't think what to put into the Novelty section.

I pondered for weeks as the days drew closer, I was getting anxious, for usually I prepared my entries well in advance. Two weeks to go and my frustration nearly saw me withdraw out of that section, when again, sleep beckoned. I felt so tired this particular afternoon that, as before, I decided to have a rest before the children came home from school and I must have begun dozing immediately.

"God I wish I knew what to put in the Castle Hill Show!" I said softly to myself, not considering for one minute that anyone could hear me.

"Why not put in a barbecue cake?" I heard my father's voice say cheerfully.

"A what?" I replied automatically.

"A barbecue cake," he said.

By this time I must have been so relaxed, because I felt like I was floating, completely unaware that I had to have begun dreaming.

"I wouldn't know how to do that!" I went on, at a loss to envisage such a cake.

Dad sighed heavily and said, "Come with me."

As dreams will go, I walked with my father through a brick, rectangular building that resembled a Santa's workshop, with what looked like elves at the benches and tables (these were all in rows), making things out of wood. I distinctly remember how we weaved our way between three rows of tables until we came to a back wall, where there was a very long and narrow table up against it.

Here, cakes and icing were everywhere. Dad smiled and pointed to a particular lump of icing and said, "Are you ready?"

"Now what am I going to do?" I asked.

"Watch carefully," he replied and despite never having made a cake in his life, nor had he ever saw my decorating skills (at least not until after his passing), he picked up the icing and proceeded to show me what to do, step by step. I was dumbfounded with his knowledge and abilities.

"But how will I make the umbrella?" I asked.

He sighed as though I was asking something that ought to have been obvious. "Like this," he said frustratingly. He picked up a saucer, turned it upside down and placed the smooth-rolled icing over it. He cut the excess off around the edge, then shaped the scalloping for the curves (the cloth area between the spokes).

"What will I use for the pole in the middle?" I asked.

He sighed heavily again. "Your number thirteen knitting needle," came the reply.

"Where on earth will I find my number thirteen knitting needle?" I wanted to know.

"In your knitting basket!" he answered with frustration.

"Where will I find the knitting basket?" I hadn't knitted for years; it could have been anywhere.

"On top of your wardrobe at the back," he said.

I felt more frustrated than him, I'm sure. He'd never seen my knitting basket before his death, so how would he know what I had in it, let alone where it was? Still confused, I said to him, "That'll never work."

He took my hand again and said, with an irritated grin, "Okay, come with me."

So I did.

We went out of this building the same way we came in and even the elves who looked at me were grinning. Going out through the front door we turned right to go to an adjacent pavilion, which looked just like the real one at the showground. He took me to the cake display cabinet and guess what was right in front of me on the middle shelf, with a First Prize and Champion ribbon beside it? My cake! I looked at Dad, beaming.

"I won! I won!" I cried in amazement, waking up at the same time. Full of excitement, I simply had to get to work on it immediately, especially with the details still so fresh in my mind.

But first I had to find the disused knitting basket. Suspicious of the dream and curious to see if it were true as well, I grabbed a chair, put it next to the wardrobe door (where I'd seen Dad's face only months earlier) and started pulling boxes down. To my surprise I found the knitting basket behind the boxes, at the back just like he'd said. I had forgotten all about it after all this time.

With much anticipation I got it down and opened it, pulling everything out, looking for the crucial needle. The basket had become something of an abyss, harbouring all sorts of junk including books, pens and chalk, besides balls of wool. Then, just when it seemed I was chasing a figment of my imagination, I had managed to scrape the bottom of the bag after clawing everything else aside. There lay the number thirteen needle – the only knitting needle in it.

I didn't know nor care where my other needles were, despite the knowledge of having a plastic lined straw knitting bag somewhere else. I was so happy, I couldn't believe it. I went straight to the kitchen and immediately started preparing the icing just the way Dad had shown me. I worked on rolling out the barbecue's 'sandstone' walls and then began the umbrella and then the rest of the cake's details and in amidst this the children came home, curious to see what I was up to.

Within five days the cake was completed, in which time I'd made a headless pig for the spit roast, with a sign that read *"Please turn me"* on its flanks, the handle for which really could be turned! There were mini rissoles on icing plates, sausages and stakes on the grid, a painted fire underneath them and a pair of tongs, scraper and a B.B.Q. fork hanging on the sandstone paver wall above.

The barbecue sat on a mock concrete flooring with a mat in front of it, a round, outdoor setting with curved seats and a mini sauce bottle on the table, with a hole in the centre of the table for guess what – the umbrella, which also had the ratchet in the middle of the now bent knitting needle! All of this lay on fake grass made out of green icing sprinkled with green jelly crystals.

When I delivered the cake on the day before the show, ready for judging, the stewards looked anxiously at it. They ushered me to the cake area and asked me to place it very carefully on the bottom shelf.

'*This doesn't look good,*' I thought. I asked if I could put the cake on the middle shelf instead, where I knew it had been displayed in the dream.

This would place it at about a metre and a half off the ground, closer to people's viewing.

"No," they said, concerned for it's safety. They were scared I might drop it or break it in the process due to my short stature. They also thought the public would see it better down on the bottom shelf. Again, I doubted my dream, as it should have been on the middle shelf to win. So I went home in despair.

The next day was Thursday; Judgement Day. I heard nothing, so I assumed it had done no good.

On the Friday my closest friend went to the show to see all the events and take in all the pavilions. That evening she rang me very excitedly, saying she had some good news for me – my cake had won First Prize, with a champion ribbon on it! I didn't believe her – couldn't believe her and thought she was simply teasing me, since the cake wasn't on the middle shelf.

So I decided not to go to the show at all because I didn't want to be disappointed and besides, not only had I other things to do on that day, I would have to return by the Sunday afternoon to collect my five entries in total. After lunch on the Sunday my heart started beating, almost excitably. I wondered if there was any truth in my friend's words. What surprises were in store for me?

I found myself wanting to go faster. Luckily my husband was driving the car that day for I feel I may have broken the speed record . . . I had become extremely anxious to get there by this point. All of a sudden I couldn't stop myself from thinking of my dream. Could it be? No it couldn't. But . . . what if?

When finally there I practically ran from the car to the pavilion, which thankfully we had been parked very close to and I dragged my family along with me, desperate to see the results. The four other cakes I'd entered had drawn me a Second and three First places, which was nice, of course. But for my 'baby', my unusual and dream-inspired barbecue novelty cake, astonishment hit me like a bullet; there was the midnight-blue First Prize ribbon, the multi-coloured Champion ribbon draped on the side and there was the cake sitting on the middle shelf – *exactly* as it had been presented in the dream.

"I won! I won!" I cried to my husband and the stewards.

"Yes," one of them said with a smile, "it was a brilliant idea, telling us to *Turn it.*"

"Thank you," I replied. "Did the judges turn it?"

"Yes," she said, very reluctantly. "You see, they really can't touch other people's cakes, in case they damage them. So they tried yours and were delighted and they thought it would be seen better on the middle shelf. Hope you don't mind?"

"No!," I replied, brimming with joy.

"Did you do it all by yourself, or did you have help?" she added encouragingly, perhaps trying to catch me out, for the rules were strict on *sole* creating.

She shouldn't have said that though because me being as excited as I was, I chimed in unthinkingly with, "Yes! My father helped me!"

She stiffened awkwardly.

"You realise you're not supposed to have any help?" she asked rather abruptly. "You're supposed to do it all by yourself."

"Oops," I replied, still in a daze. "Oh yes, I know, but Dad's been dead ten years!"

Well, this left her looking like the proverbial stunned mullet. Her face changed with something of a blend of shock and horror – how could she explain *that* to the judges? With that we packed up my cakes and ribbons and went back home, feeling all smug and content. I was thanking my beautiful father all the way, grateful now for his 'special' inspiration. Knowing now that life *did* exist beyond physical death, this experience gave me the best feeling I'd ever had . . . and it changed my life forever.

∞

The prize-winning B.B.Q. cake, spiritually assisted by my Dad

The Champion and First Place Ribbons awarded to me for the B.B.Q. cake

Chapter Three

EARLY ENCOUNTERS

My Wish Card

Around 1974, a very close and dear friend of my mother's came from England to visit with her. We called and treated her, as an Aunty, because we knew her from a very young age, only what I didn't know at the time was that she could read ordinary playing cards (whereas many psychics typically work with illustrated Tarot cards). During this six-week Australian holiday, my husband and I invited Aunty May over to our place for the weekend. This is when Mum told me what she did.

"Would you like me to read your cards for you?" Aunty May had asked me.

Considering I was now already well interested in the 'unknown', I said yes quite happily. Having seen and heard of other people who had done readings, I thought it would be fun and I had wished that one day I, too, might be able to read cards in the future. I never told anyone this at the time as I was led to believe you had to be born with the knowledge, for which you had inherited the gift from a family member. Thankfully this wasn't so, as I found out.

After she finished reading my cards (which she was very good at) Aunty May said to me, "Pick out twenty-six cards and make a wish." She went on to say, "And if the wish card comes out, I'll tell you what you wished for."

My adopted aunty read my cards really well, but when she came to the last one, which happened to be the Wish Card, she stated so many things she thought I had wished for – which I hadn't – so she gave in.

"I give up," she uttered. "What did you wish for?"

I smiled, it was obvious.

"I wished I could do what you're doing – read cards," I replied.

She looked relieved.

"Oh, is that all? I can teach you that before I go back home!"

And so before returning to England, she had given me her list of meanings to each playing card and showed me how to read the 'mock' stories and told me to study hard. 'Mock' stories are where you pretend to read for an imaginary person – or the sitter as they are called (in due course) – and you shuffle the deck, select and read the cards, as if the sitter has chosen them. Then you piece together 'their' story as it appears to you from the spread, according to the order and placement of each card (most tarot deck books will tell you the various ways to lay out the cards, however in this case, I had to learn which way the plain deck of cards should be laid out and read. The method I used became very successful for me over the years).

"Ask friends to be guinea pigs," she'd said. "And learn from *them* whether you're on the right track or not."

Five years after dad died, I studied very long and hard into how to meditate and communicate with the Spirit World by going to the Parramatta Spiritualist Church and joining into what is known as an open circle. I gained a lot there, such as how to heal the body with Spirit energy, or why the importance of protecting oneself psychically and mentally could make a difference when dealing with malicious entities, or, as is frequent enough, working or learning within the company of ego-driven people.

So from the circles at the church, I gained the awareness of how to properly meditate and of how to listen to the inner voices in my head that were coming from Spirit (which are different to the voices a Schizophrenic sufferer receives). I felt that now I was beginning to understand how this 'other' world worked through us.

80C3

The Anxious Sister

Some six months on and one morning I was preparing my children's breakfast and making their lunches, standing at the bench top between the kitchen and the dining room, when I saw this beautiful lady with striking-coloured hair; reddish, almost copper in shade. She was stunning and mentally I asked who she was and what did she want with me.

"Could you ring Fay up right away?" she asked with some urgency. Fay was a close friend at the time, who lived only a few streets from me.

'It would be too early to ring her now. She would be busy getting her boys ready for school,' I replied to her. *'I will ring her in a little while.'*

This was not good enough, apparently, for she showed me a vision of Fay looking sad while getting her boys ready for school. She had a tear in her eye and the spirit-woman explained that it would be too late for Fay if I were to leave it until later.

"Ring her *now*," she insisted, "because she will be going out very soon, as Mum is very ill!"

I decided to ring Fay immediately, for I could have a problem with this woman if I didn't. "Sorry to call you, Fay," I began awkwardly. "If it's a bad time I'll ring you later."

"Oh no, that's okay," she said. "I'm just about to go out to visit Mum."

"Have you been crying because your Mum's very ill?" I asked, hoping I wasn't intruding.

"How on earth did you know?" she replied in a shocked voice.

"There's a lady who's standing in front of me with reddish hair," I explained.

Fay didn't know about my spiritual interests before this. Cautiously I described the ghost-lady in detail, feeling a need to explain the reason for my spur-of-the-moment call.

Fay gasped. "Are you sure? How old does she look?"

"Around thirty-ish." I gave her some other details about this woman, too.

She paused for a few minutes and then said, "That sounds like my older sister, but she died a few years ago."

After a moment I continued.

"She told me about you going out soon to see your mother. She showed me a vision of you crying and said that your mother was ill."

Fay went quiet.

I attempted to comfort her by relaying the spirit's message. "Don't worry about Mum, she will be o.k., but she'll need a lot of care."

By now the ghost lady had started to fade. Fay couldn't thank me enough.

"That's great news!" she said. "Next time you come around I'll show you her photo."

When we finally hung up, I knew she was feeling a lot happier.

The next week I went to see her at her home and she showed me her sister's photo as promised and as a developing psychic, it was rewarding.

"Yes," I said with a smile, "That was the lady I saw in my dining room alright."

Fay smiled too. "Funny," she said, "just before you rang me that morning I remembered thinking of her, wishing she was here to talk to. Then you rang – it felt like she was talking to me through you. I was so pleased. It made me feel really good because I'm sure that with the way I was feeling then, I could have had an accident on my way to see Mum!"

From this encounter, I was now more convinced that spirits can be sent to help us in lots of ways and often we may never realise the extent to which this help may reach. I was never frightened or worried of the concept of "ghosts" any more after that, with the exception of this next one particular individual, who proved to be quite scary indeed . . .

ഓൽ

The Very Angry Ghost

Although I had decided I would never be frightened or worried of spirits – or 'ghosts', as they are often called – there was one particular individual who honestly scared me and I would not wish this kind of experience on any beginner in the psychic fields.

I was attending my very first paid session at a client's house about twenty minutes drive from my home. We'll call her Anne. Anne booked me for seven o'clock and I was on top of the world as I was just getting really good at reading the cards and at listening to Spirit talking to me. Contrary to many television shows and movies, 'ghosts' cannot harm you and I believed firmly in the protection of my spirit guides and my spirit loved ones being with me.

My oldest daughter, Debbie, who was in her mid-teens and learning psychometry wanted to come along too. She needed the experience and I looked forward to seeing how her performance would go. I didn't mind because the invited guests attending the session would play as "guinea pigs" for her while waiting for their private card readings with me.

Armed with complete trust in my guides, whose judgement would help me to speak truthfully by telling me what to say, I felt that I was strong enough to tackle anything or anyone and it never occurred to me that my first real 'case' might be a spirit with an attitude.

The evening had a scary atmosphere to begin with and as I approached the area where Anne lived, I remembered her telling me to, "come around the back streets and down a laneway behind the shops", not realising she was in a rough neighbourhood. Thank God for headlights, because the laneway was very dark and I was feeling very uncomfortable. I started praying for safety and security and help to find the right place without delay.

We finally arrived at the building Anne had described; one little light was on at the top of a steep metal stairway. I hated stairs, especially metal ones and she must have been looking out of the rear window for me. As

I drove into her drive and stopped, she opened her back door and called down to me to come on up.

"I'm sorry for bringing you in the back door," she said on our arrival at the top of the landing, "I live above the shops and this is the only way into my place."

I introduced my daughter and told Anne what Debbie would like to do in regards to advancing her psychometry training, which she quite happily agreed with and we were taken inside. She led my daughter to a small table in her lounge room, round the corner from where I was to sit but also where I could keep an eye on her if need be. Anne then showed me to the kitchen table on which I was going to read from and introduced me to her mother.

With the preliminaries out of the way, I sat down to read for Anne, who wanted her reading done first, ahead of her mother, or before her guests arrived. I only just barely had her shuffle her cards and began laying them out when I noticed a tall lady and a small child of around eight years old walking through the back door. They were dressed in older-style clothes and went across the lounge room floor in front of me, seemingly headed for the front of the house, where I lost sight of them.

Moments later, they came back and on passing the kitchen area where I sat, they looked at me and smiled.

"Oh, hello," I said to them, smiling in return.

"Who are you talking to?" Anne asked.

"That lady and the little girl," I replied. "They must be the early birds, because I didn't hear them come in."

The woman and little girl continued on their way to the back door, disappearing as they walked right through it.

"But you are the only ones here so far," she said. "No one else has turned up yet."

Then I explained to her at what I had just seen.

"The lady with the little girl – just walked in then turned around and went back out again. I thought she must have been an early arrival but they didn't speak. They just smiled at me, then they disappeared through the back door."

"Oh!" she said excitedly. "Did you really see someone?"

"Yes," I said and went on to describe what they looked like.

Anne sighed with relief. "They are the resident ghosts," she explained. "They live here and won't harm you. A lot of people have seen them in the past few years. They were killed in that room near where your daughter is sitting. They used to own the butcher shop below us and one day the husband went mad and killed them in a frenzy. But they don't worry us. We're used to them now."

My blood ran cold and I gulped.

"Oops," I uttered quietly, feeling very awkward. Although the encounter left a weird sensation in me, I proceeded on with reading the lady's cards, which unfolded without further incident, aside from the arrival of some of her guests. When I had finished the session with her she was both happy and relieved and couldn't wait to tell them what I had seen and "how good I was," as she had put it. She also told them of my daughter's ambitions and they were happy to "give her a go" while waiting for their turn with me.

As one woman put it, "Two readings for the price of one – not bad!"

Unfortunately for me, the worst was still to come.

𝜀𝜗𝜁ℬ

Her elderly mother – who we'll refer to as Gladys – sat down for my next reading, which was to be my biggest challenge yet and she came with a *very* angry spirit. And I mean angry! As she shuffled the cards and I settled down to read them, I became aware of another presence around me, but couldn't see anyone.

She placed them into nine stacks on the table as instructed and with each stack in turn, I proceeded to turn the cards face up, one at a time in a line. I noticed a pair of shoes on the floor beside my right foot; men's shoes, however I was determined to keep my focus on the cards.

My first sign of trouble was when I saw the Death card and the King of Spades right in the middle of the pack, laying next to each other (the King of Spades usually represents a dark-haired man; the death card does not always represent a factual death, though in this case, it did).

'*This doesn't look good*', I thought to myself, not knowing whether I should say to Gladys, "You are going to hear of a death," or, "There has been a death."

As I placed the last card from the pack down and then glanced up to the first card at the top of the first row to see what I could find to tell her, the pair of feet became agitated; the right foot was tapping with impatience. Suddenly all hell broke loose; not one card had a picture of any kind to it. They had all turned blank – quite literally.

36

They were all as white as a sheet to me and I thought there was something wrong with my eyes, for I couldn't see any story for her – past, present *or* future.

I said to myself, '*Come on, you've got to say something! This lady is expecting a reading and I can't let her down*'.

The foot-tapping became vigorous, sending a chill up my spine. I cringed and *really* started to worry. So much that it bothered me – I feared this 'ghost' might attack me (like you see in the movies): I feared the unknown. I couldn't read anything, but by golly, I *felt something*!

Not wanting to frighten the lady even though *I* was quite terrified, I was determined to carry on, pretending nothing was wrong. I let my eyes scan up his black, pin-striped and stocky body, realising very quickly that if I didn't do something immediately, he would. He reminded me of a Mafia-type personality, with his strong Greek, or Italian, presence. His waistline came into view and his fist was shaking rudely at me.

"Come on, hurry up! Say something!" his gruff voice demanded. "Read her bloody cards if you can! You said you could!" His sarcasm and arrogance . . . his whole manner was unbearable!

By now the inside of my entire body felt like a whirlpool, my head spinning in wild circles, though I was to learn my sitter was not aware of this inner turmoil. Stubbornly I kept my eyes on the cards and mentally said to him; '*No, you're not going to frighten me! I will not be bullied, even by you!*'

"Come on, you said you could read her bloody cards!" he insisted grumpily. "Now *read* them! I want to hear what you've got to say to her!"

Some five minutes must have passed for the woman who was patiently waiting opposite me, blissfully unaware of the harrowing monster, whose foot had increased it's aggressive tapping. I decided that I had to take control of the situation, compose my fear and 'attack' back at him.

'*Are you her husband*?' I mentally asked him.

"So what if I am?" he replied nastily. "It's none of your bloody business – now just read her bloody cards!"

Despite his heated response I felt a little bit more at ease, for I knew then which way I was heading. I looked at Gladys and apologised for the delay, which must have seemed a long time for her.

"That's okay," she said, still oblivious of the man. "Not to worry."

"Has your husband passed over?" I directly asked.

"Oh *yes*, thank God!" she said with great relief, yet which also seemed to carry deep resentment.

"Was he a very impatient man?" I enquired.

"The worst possible kind!" she said. "Why? Don't tell me he's here?"

"Yes, he won't let me read the cards properly. That's why it's taking me so long, as he is being a bully to me," I explained.

"That would be right, he had no time for this kind of stuff."

I calmed down a little then.

"Now I know what I'm dealing with," I said to her, then pointed to an armchair in the lounge room nearby – opposite to where my daughter sat. I stared pointedly at the husband. "I'm not going to read these cards until you go and sit down over there!"

"Oh *okay*," he grumbled and with lot's of moaning and grunting, he reluctantly went shuffling over to the chair. Calmly I looked down at the cards and it's hardly surprising to say that all of them had their printed faces back!

Halfway through the reading, the mother asked me if he was still in the chair, to which I looked and to my amazement, he was. I was able to describe how and what, he was doing; he had a can of beer in his right hand, draped over the arm of the chair and he appeared very sleepy, with his head nodding off.

"That'd be right," she said unsurprised. "That's exactly what he would do when he was alive." By the end of her reading he was gone and I was so relieved. Gladys thanked me and moved into the lounge beside her daughter, no doubt to tell her of her fathers visit.

⁎⁍⁑

My daughter, meanwhile, had given psychometry readings for three very happy ladies and I heard them talking about what she had said to them. I also heard a lot of children laughing and behaving very stupidly. She laughed with them and I began to realise that her voice had become excitable and incomprehensible.

"What's going on?" I called to her, concerned for her well-being. I knew there were no kids in the group of people who were there, so I focused my thoughts around her to discover she had seven spirit kids with her, ranging from ten years of age, to about sixteen years old.

"I don't know," she replied. No one else could see or hear these children, except for her and I.

"Who are the children you're talking to?" I asked.

"Don't know," she answered. "These kids are telling me what to say. They want me to tell this lady [her fourth sitter] to go to the lolly shop and steal some lollies from it."

This left me feeling very uncomfortable again. Because I was still reeling from my own ordeal with the man in the armchair, I 'saw red' at the way these children were carrying on, making so much noise and likely misleading Debbie.

"Send them away," I firmly insisted.

"They won't go," she said.

Angry and armed with the attitude of being ready for anything, of thinking that no one was going to get to me the wrong way again, I called back to her and said, "Tell them that if they don't go away, I'll stop you from doing anymore readings."

The "ghost children" got very stroppy with this.

"Oh come on fellas," the oldest one sarcastically said, "let's go. It's not going to be fun anymore with *her* around."

He meant me, of course and with that remark they disappeared through the wall. I then told Debbie to sit down and not to do any more readings for the rest of the night as I didn't want to have any more bad entities coming through. The rest of the evening went well after that and about three hours later we were happy to be going home, knowing our customers were very pleased with us – especially Anne and her mother.

ଽଠ୯ଓ

The following Sunday evening I went to the spiritualist church and a great elderly medium lady was on the platform. When the service came to a close with people going home and before she went to have a cup of tea in the kitchen, I approached her, telling her of my terrifying ordeal two nights earlier. Since I'd never had that experience before, I wanted to know how I should have handled the man and the children.

"From what you have just described to me, you did everything just right," she confidently said. "You never let them get the better of you and you treated them like spoilt children. You have to be in control at all times

39

and show them you are not frightened of them even when you are. But most of all, *always* ask for protection before you start your readings."

She went on to say that we (the readers) must take control of our emotions and never let them get the better of us. "Treat bad spirits like out-of-control children and let them know you're the boss," she said. "You did great considering they did what you asked of them and they left peacefully. Congratulations."

I was so pleased with this outcome, but more relieved to know I was on the right path in my spiritual journey.

&

The Surprise Wedding

I had many wonderful readings after this and more people heard about me and asked if they could come to my home. I didn't mind back then because this way I wasn't leaving my husband to look after our four children while I went out by myself at night. When customers came for their readings, he could go out into the garage and work on his projects and the children would watch T.V. for up to an hour before going to bed. Most of the time my visitors watched the T.V. with them (when they came in groups). My regular visits to the spirit-circle gave me great comfort and I learned how to control my thoughts there with practice.

One particular evening five people had driven an hour from Sydney's inner suburbs to share in a group reading, where they sat around the table together. They were obviously all close friends and quite comfortable with hearing one another's messages. We worked it so that as I would finish reading for the person on my right, they would all get up and change seats to the next person in the line, a little like playing musical chairs.

Comments would be aired among them with each session, saying how good and how accurate I was. My next lady shuffled the cards and placed them face-down on the table. When I turned them over, the marriage card was prominent. Both she and the lady beside her were fair-haired and the card I saw beside the marriage card was the Queen of Hearts. Close to these two was the travel card, so I knew they were all linked.

"Are you planning to get married soon?" I asked her.

"Of course not," was the answer.

"Are you planning an overseas trip?" I asked, "Or have you just come back from one?"

"No," she replied, looking puzzled.

"Well, I can see an overseas trip for a fair lady here, or she has just returned from one."

Sue looked at the blond woman sitting next to her, who was in line to be read for next and who, unknown to me, was one of her siblings.

41

"Could this be a sister of mine?" she asked.

"Quite possibly. It'll be someone who is very close to you," I replied. "I can see a marriage around her."

They laughed as though the idea was absurd.

"Oh no," the sister said. "She hasn't even got a boyfriend yet!"

"There is a dark-headed man involved with this woman," I said, indicating the King of Clubs, (usually meaning a warm, loving man). "He is a little older than her and it looks like he's coming from overseas to marry her."

Sue grinned at her sibling and said, "I wonder if it is our older sister? She's just returned home from an overseas holiday and bragged on about this man she had met."

"Maybe she found someone and is possibly going to surprise you," I suggested, for clearly they did not seem to accept the 'unlikely' news. "This woman here," I went on, pointing to the Queen's card, "is planning a wedding very soon; within a ten. It might be ten weeks, but I feel it will be more like ten months."

I felt I could not tell them just when, exactly, I *could* see it happening, for in my spirit-vision the man was definitely coming into her life; he had dark-hair, was a little older and was travelling over water. But I also could hear my guides telling me what to say and *they* didn't lie. Would I frighten them if I were to spell it out in such detail? Sure people love to hear about ghost stories and they always seem to enjoy learning about a deceased loved one being near them, however to describe the message in its entirety could sometimes prove to be an unnerving thing.

So I left it at that and continued with the rest of the session, thinking this would be all there was to hear of the matter. In due course we moved along to her sibling and no further reference or indication from the cards regarding the mysterious wedding came through.

Marie was the last to sit before me; a tallish lady who looked worried. I had the inkling she was hoping I could help her with a certain problem. In fact, it seemed like someone in spirit immediately began tuning into my thoughts as I opened our session, for an elderly lady appeared in the room, whom I saw from out of the right corner of my eye.

She was a plump sort of lady who was sitting at one of my sewing machines positioned near the back door of my home and she was drinking out of a beautiful China cup and saucer whilst apparently talking to an old fashioned-looking man now standing next to her. He wore a dark, pin-striped suit and held a small glass – with whiskey in it, I sensed.

I usually like to wait before talking about the cards to give the visiting spirit, or spirits, a chance to speak first. But neither of them took any notice of me. They appeared too engrossed in their own conversation, so I read on as though they were merely background company at a social gathering.

The Ace of Clubs came to me first – the card linked to property.

"You're looking at selling something, possibly a house, or maybe some property?" I said.

"Yes," she answered.

"It's interesting that it's come up first," I remarked, still waiting for either of the couple to say something. The meaning of the card wasn't clear to me and on reflection, I suspect this may have had something to do with Marie's own confusion, for I was soon to learn that it was a difficult decision for her to make. "But we'll see what comes of it later in the cards," I added, when nothing was offered by the spirits. I finished the reading shortly after and asked if any of it had made sense.

"Yes, all of it," she answered.

The happily chatting couple did not fade away as will happen when a client's messages are complete, so their continued presence probably meant there was a need for further communication with her. I knew, too, not all had been answered for her.

"Do you have any questions," I enquired, "as I have two people in spirit with us and I don't know who they are?"

The 'ghost lady' looked at me and smiled and it seemed she mouthed the word 'Mother', or 'Mother's sister'. I felt encouraged to continue in that direction.

"Do you have a mother or maybe an aunty that has passed over?" I added, which brought a confirmed response from Marie.

"Yes," she said. "My aunt died two years ago. Why, is that in the cards?"

"No, she is sitting over there," I replied and pointed to my sewing machine. "She loved her cups of tea didn't she?"

With a stunned look, she said, "Yes . . ."

"Do you have an uncle or a grandfather who loved his whisky on the other side too?"

"Yes, my uncle died when I was in my late teens," she explained. "He was the aunt's husband. Can you really see them?"

"Yes," I said, with a cheeky grin on my face. It felt so good to be able to see them and not be frightened of them. The lady went on to explain to me how the couple had owned a general store when they were alive, but had left it to her when they had passed over. Finally the difficult question came out.

"Could you ask them if it is okay to sell it, as it is getting too much for me to manage by myself?" she asked, "With the big stores moving into the area they are pricing me out of business. I want their permission to sell it."

"Ask them yourself, they can hear you," I replied. "Just listen to your thoughts for the answer."

Of course, she couldn't hear them for she didn't know how to. I tried to show her the way to focus, but it was to no avail. In the end I had to give her their answer.

"Yes, [they'd said] go for it love. We understand that you can't win with developers."

The group around the table were all amazed; how could I see and hear their loving spirits? And yet, their presence and messages gave them hope. Relieved, Marie knew she could sell the shop inherited from her aunt and uncle without feeling guilty and as for Sue, well, a chat with her sister was inevitable. They left and I retired to bed, pleased with the connections I'd made for them and ready for sleep.

Not quite late the next morning I received a phone call from a rather angry lady, whose voice I did not recognise.

"Hello," I said.

"You bitch!" she shouted. "You spoilt my surprise!"

"What are you talking about?" I said, caught unawares. "What surprise?"

"My wedding surprise!" she replied. "My boyfriend is arriving from England in about six weeks and I was going to tell the family of our plans *after* he had settled in!"

The penny dropped.

"You must be Sue's sister, the lady I read cards for last night. She said it might have been about you."

"That's right," she snapped, "It was about me. But how did you know?"

"Because it was there in the cards," I explained. "I saw a fair lady with the travel card. She had a dark-haired man with her and I could see that he was coming to you from over some water. He was a little older than you and the Seven of Diamonds was connected to him. That's the card that told me you were planning to marry him. I'm sorry if I upset you. It wasn't intentional."

She seemed to calm down and perhaps sensibility had returned, for she said, "Yeah, well my sister told me how good you were. They had a great night, she said." She paused very briefly and in a more settled mood she asked, "If it's possible, could I please come for a reading to see if I will be happy and if I am doing the right thing?"

I had to smile at that.

"Yes, if you want to," I answered. "When would be a good time for you?"

We made a day to suit us both for the very next week. All went well; she was to have a very happy marriage and children, too, I think, but with this being so long ago for me, I cannot honestly remember the details.

৪৩

Chapter Four

CLIENT READINGS

A Mischievous Spirit

One evening I was preparing to attend the open circle at the Parramatta spiritualist church, when my daughter, Debbie asked if she could come with me. She had been once before and all had gone well then, but tonight was going to be different.

We found our places in the [meditation] circle, with Debbie sitting next to an elderly lady four chairs from me. Once meditation began and I had started to relax, the sound of someone sobbing came from Debbie's area and on bringing myself 'out', I saw that it was her.

I waited a few minutes to see if she would settle down, but no, she only became louder. Unsure if she was doing this for attention or because it was possible she'd had a 'bad' spirit in her, I intervened, feeling I couldn't take any chances at this early stage of her development. Being new at this sort of thing, she wouldn't have known how to handle any sorts of 'possession', good or bad, so I quietly got up and tip-toed over to her.

Gently I put my arms around her shoulders and whispered to her to "let it go". This proved to be a fruitless cause and so, with as little disruption to the other people of our circle, I eased her from her chair and said, "Come with me," and led her to the only door that opened into, or out of, the hall.

Four steps fronted the church with the top step – or landing – barely having enough room for one person to stand on, let alone two of us. I closed the door quietly as a light sprinkling of rain came down, which caught me by surprise, for it had been a clear sky on our initial arrival and even then, still no clouds were visible. In fact, moonlight shone over the street lights. Perhaps someone had put a sprinkler on our faces? Of course not, but the thoughts raced through my mind because by now I was feeling very uncomfortable.

I found myself sniffing the still air, which smelled strange. Automatically I started praying quietly to God to keep us safe from harm and to take away any evil spirits that might have been around us. As I uttered the word "around", the huge white flash of a lightning bolt hit Debbie in her forehead. It was incredibly bright, yet I saw this spirit fly back as though it was sucked right out of her body and up into the universe. Had I not seen this happen with my own eyes, I would never have believed anyone telling me about it.

By now the air smelled 'pure' and believe it or not, the fine rainfall had stopped, with the sky just as clear as when we had arrived.

I asked Debbie how she felt.

"Good," she said, "but what are we doing outside?"

It seemed she did not realise what had just occurred. I briefed her of the situation and asked her if she would like to return inside.

"Yes," came the reply.

Quietly we re-entered the darkened hall and tip toed straight across to the kitchen to wait until everyone came out of their meditation. Although she seemed shaken, it was evident she had not suffered undue physical effects. It was yet another experience which illustrated to me the importance of calling upon divine protection before attempting psychic-related experiences.

∽∾

The Readings in Church

While still in the learning stages of how to tune in to the spirit world, I was asked if I would like to help out with platform duties on the Sunday night's church services. This involved introducing the hymns for the service as well as announcing the guest mediums who would perform readings for the assembly.

I wasn't used to public speaking, which would, as I knew, mean speaking to an audience; one-to-one readings across a table was quite different from standing on a stage in front of a crowd. However, I thought it might be interesting to try and did my best to overcome my nerves on the night.

Things happen for a reason – always.

You see, while the trained psychics were performing their open readings, I too, was seeing spirits walking around the crowded hall. They were asking me to pass on messages to their loved ones who were waiting in the audience, because those people were going to miss out on a reading from the professional mediums.

This caught me unprepared and at first I didn't want to speak up for fear of intruding upon an area for which I had no business. I was only meant to *present* the mediums and hymns on the platform, not *read* for anyone. But the spirit people insisted for me to speak to their families – whom they were drawing my attention to – saying that I would be the only other person there who could do it and that the guest mediums would understand and thus wouldn't be upset with me.

At last I agreed. '*Okay*,' I mentally replied. '*I'll see what I can do – but you'll have to tell me what to say!*'

'*Just start talking to the families and we'll do the rest*,' they assured.

'*Thank you*,' I replied and left it at that, hoping they really would come through as promised.

As the mediums finally finished their presentations, I noticed the specific three family groups the spirits had pointed to earlier did not, indeed, receive any readings.

Duty called for me to now thank our special guests for coming along and then to close the service with a prayer, but I didn't. Instead, going 'against the rules', I turned to the psychics, thanked them, then apologised for being rude but, "Would you mind me doing three more readings, as I have three spirits desperately wanting me to talk to their families? Apparently there's something they need to hear."

Aware I was new at this, they smiled humorously, their palms raised toward the crowd. "You go for it, Love," they said pleasantly enough and, "We understand."

This made me feel a whole lot better, although in truth, I don't think they were very happy with me about it. I hoped I wasn't set to make a fool of myself. I relaxed and sent up a mental prayer for the spirits to guide me and to help me as they'd promised they would. Then, giving it my best shot, I looked around the hall for the audience member who was to get the first of these messages.

I was drawn to the lady in the back row of the right-hand corner, where a patiently-waiting male spirit was holding a banana bunch over her head. She looked so sad and lonely and pointing to her, I listened to what this man had to say.

"Do you know anyone in Coffs Harbour?" I asked her, for he was telling me of her going there. "Are you planning a holiday there soon, or in the near future? Or maybe are you planning to move there?"

She replied by saying that she did know someone in this town, but that she couldn't make up her mind about what to do in regards to visiting the place and that the decision had been bothering her for some time.

"You have a male person in spirit behind you holding a bunch of bananas over your head," I explained and described to her what he looked like. "He said that you have been depressed lately. He is telling me to tell you that you will be moving up there very soon and not to be frightened because it will be a good move. He will be watching over you."

A big smile filled her face.

"Thank you," she said. "Someone very close to me passed over last year and that sounds just like him. You have just helped me with a problem I couldn't solve myself."

I never saw that lady at the church again and I presume her move to Coffs Harbour came around rather quickly as a result.

My next spirit stood behind this lovely couple in the second row right in front of me.

I indicated to them and said, "I have an elderly lady behind you, which I feel may have been a grandmother to one of you. I don't know who she is with as she is standing between the both of you; her left arm is around the man's shoulders and her right hand [pointing to the lady beside him] is rubbing your back very gently." I then addressed this lady. "Do you have a backache or some kind of pain in that area and do you feel warm between your shoulders? Do you understand me please?"

"Yes," she said. "I suffer with a bad back and it sounds like it may be my grandmother."

After describing what she looked like I asked, "Were you very close to this grandmother?"

"Yes," she replied. "She was my favourite Nanna, because she understood me more than anybody."

"Why is she with the man next to you?" I asked.

"Because this is my husband and they were very close to each other. She admired him and thought the world of him."

The Nanna-spirit showed me a heart-shaped, gold locket, so I asked the lady if she had one of this description.

"Yes," came the answer, with some astonishment. "I only looked at it the other day. It's in my dresser draw."

"Did your Nanna give it to you?"

Shock registered on her face. "Yes," she said.

"Do you get depressed a lot?"

"Yes, why?"

"Your Nanna wants you to wear your locket whenever you are feeling down or very depressed and you are to think of her at the same time. Do you ever smell roses around you at all?"

"Nearly all the time," she whispered, glancing around her as though the smell was with her as we spoke. "They were Nan's favourite flower. She had them in her garden. I can even smell them now."

"That's because she is giving you a bunch of roses right now and is always with you when you need her most. Whenever you smell roses, it means she is telling you that she is around and to just think of her. She is also trying to heal your back pain and is giving you a lot of love."

She was very happy and thanked me. I turned to her husband and felt the depression was also around him.

"Are you also depressed?" I asked him,

"Yes," he replied.

"Is it because you are out of work? Are you finding it hard to get a job?" I queried.

"Yes," he answered, "but how did you know that?"

"Because her Nanna is telling me. Would you take anything offered to you?" I asked, referring to employment opportunities.

"Possibly. What are you suggesting?" he said.

"Do you like motorbikes?" I asked.

"Yes, why?"

"Because her Nanna is showing me one like the Posties use. Have you ever thought of being a postman?" I said.

He was nodding. "I have the form but wasn't sure wether to fill it out in case I failed the test." He hesitated and then added, "I couldn't handle another rejection."

"No, you won't fail this one because Nanna is going to be there to help you get through it," I answered. "Fill it out as soon as possible and you will get the job very soon. Go with your gut feeling."

He smiled very happily. "Thank you so much," he said. "This reading is just what I needed to hear."

"You're welcome," I replied, smiling back. "God bless you both."

I then looked down to the rear-left corner of the room, amazed and reminded again at how crowded the church was – with many physical people and quite a number of spirit people. I'd never seen the hall so full before and it was a little sad, because I couldn't give them all a reading this night.

The last spirit I was to assist stood waiting for me very patiently next to a rather attractive woman, who was sitting on the edge of a very small stage in the back section of the hall. This reading, for me, was the best one, for his loved one was moved to tears of joy.

The well-dressed spirit man was holding a guitar and singing *Danny Boy* to the lady. I was sorry no-one else could hear him, as he had a beautiful voice and I told him so.

'*Yeah*', he said to me, '*but I never used to be this good. She used to laugh at me and think I was dreadful, but I was only learning then*'.

"Did you know of a young man who was learning the guitar before he passed over?" I asked the lady.

She sat up very straight and looked around to the person beside and behind her, apparently unsure if it was she I was talking to.

"Yes, you," I said, looking at her, "the lady on the corner."

"Yes," she replied very nervously. "My nephew."

"Did he try singing the song *Danny Boy* to you?"

She chuckled. "Oh yes," she said with a grin.

"He wasn't very good at it, was he?"

"No!" she said, laughing it off. "He was terrible. I used to tell him that."

"Have you ever thought you could hear him singing to you?"

A frown creased her forehead. "Not really."

"It's a pity because he has a beautiful voice and he plays the guitar very well. He's singing *Danny Boy* to you right now."

The woman went dead quiet and her eyes began to fill with tears. Profound silence filled the room in which the drop of a pin could've been heard.

I went on gently. "He's saying to tell you that, "I've learned all the words now Aunty. You'd be proud of me"."

She started to cry and I apologised for upsetting her.

"No, it's okay," she said. "But I miss him terribly."

"He is always with you and is giving you a lot of love. When you're quiet and relaxed, listen carefully as you may even hear him singing or talking to you. Never dismiss that sense of him speaking to you in your head. Just go with the flow and follow your heart."

"Thank you," she replied, looking much brighter now.

I looked over at the guest mediums, who sat very quietly to my right and I apologised to them again for being rude at intervening their sessions. Yet they were amazed, it seemed.

"No," one of them said decisively. "It was meant for those people to hear what you had received and we're proud that you acknowledged them. You must always give what you are given in these circumstances, even if it doesn't make any sense to you. But it might make a big difference to them."

Their words were the approval I needed, so I went on to close the service with a prayer of thanks and love, knowing I had done the right thing by all. Afterwards, many of those in the church committee came up and praised my actions, including the two psychic guests. The four people for whom I had passed on the spirits' messages met up with me, too and said that they couldn't believe it had been my very first public reading. I have to say that it was an exciting moment in my life and I felt 'on top of the world'.

A few weeks later I was asked to share the platform again with another learner; she read by holding a flower supplied by an audience member. Although I hadn't tried that form of psychometry before, I did clairvoyant work with about ten people that night and hoped I had been right with the messages that came through. There were no complaints and a lot of joyful smiles, so all, apparently, had gone well.

80C3

The Bag Sale

Also around this time I was asked to go to a shopping arcade in Sydney some forty minutes drive from home. A store there was having a big hand bag promotion and offered to pay me to read for their customers. The deal was that for those who bought their bags, they would receive a free reading with a psychic.

The pay was a terrific boost to our family's budget, despite being tucked into a pokey corner downstairs and 'out of sight'. It was rather spooky in there, actually, as the shop's basement reminded me of a dungeon, with no windows, in utter silence, without any sight of a staff member the whole time. Racks of clothes surrounded me and my tiny table and I guess this was a first for the retail industry, since the mystical 'fortune-teller' did not work out of shops in those days. Indeed, I had never advertised my name back then for fear it was an illegal practice – such was the public stigma toward the subject.

I had a young lady who, although wasn't showing signs of stress, must have been feeling it, for I felt it as an energy around her, as well as within me, too. She shuffled the card deck and while I placed them into their positions, ready to read, a man appeared at her left side. He was very handsome and he held a small baby in his arms.

"Have you lost your father," I asked.

"Yes," came the answer.

"I also see a little baby. Did you lose that too?"

Her eyes filled tearfully right away. "Yes," she whispered.

"Was it a boy?"

"Yes, he was only five months old."

"Don't worry about him being alone," I said, "Because Dad is looking after him."

"Can you see that in the cards?" she asked. This was becoming a frequent question, I noticed.

"No," I replied and pointed to her left arm. "Dad is holding him right beside you. They are both fine."

She went on to explain that these two had died about eighteen months apart, first with her father and then with the baby. She was understandably devastated and now felt so lonely without them.

'*Tell her not to worry about the baby,*' her dad said to me, '*Tell her not to worry about tomorrow, I'll always be with her to help her out where ever it is possible. The future will get better for her. Let her know that we'll always be by her side. We love her and will be there for support as much as possible. Her son is fine and well.*'

I passed the message on as given to me and she drew immense comfort with the reassurance and existence of her deceased loved ones. I noticed her stress had partially lifted with the closure of the reading and the pressure-anxiety I had experienced inside of me was no longer there.

I honestly cannot recall the other readings I had given in that store, some thirty years ago now, but by the end of that week I was certainly ready for a rest. The manager came down to thank me, saying that they had done extremely well with the promotion. They were interested to know if I would do this with them again if they repeated the scheme, to which I agreed, eagerly to strengthen my spiritual development, though they had not, apparently, decided to do any more promotions, for the call never came.

෮෮෮

The Sweet-toothed Spirit

A month or so later, Margaret and Bob, an elderly couple from the church committee asked me to make their sixtieth wedding anniversary cake. It was only to be a small affair, so they wanted a simple cake with two large sugar bells on it (bell-shaped cake decorations made of white sugar). I had become known for my skill in making and decorating cakes for special occasions, so we examined some photographs from my cake albums for ideas and selected a design in which flowers were to be laid as though trailing from inside of the bells.

In those first three weeks I would give the couple updates when I saw them of a Sunday evening at church, to let them know of the cake's progress: the cake is baked, ready for the icing, or, the icing is on, waiting for the decorations etc. Unfortunately not much progress was happening when and where it was needed most regarding the sugar bells. From the start of making the bells I experienced problems I had otherwise never encountered before. Making the bells consists of mixing together sugar and egg white and pressing this damp blend into a mould – in this case, the shape of a church bell. In the drying process I then hollow out the centre mix and wait for the rest to set. Several hours can go into the creation of these ornaments and if not handled with care, they are fragile and will break easily.

Well, the first bell came out perfectly, nice and firm and ready for positioning on the cake. Unfortunately the second bell broke apart. I made a third bell to replace the broken one but it, too, crumbled apart. Annoyed, I crafted a fourth bell and on removing it from the mould, I groaned when the sugar collapsed in my hand. Actually, if I'm being honest, I swore . . .

I couldn't understand why the mate of this bell would not come together, no matter how many additional replacements I prepared. Time was getting away on me – two weeks had passed and the delivery date loomed too, too closely. The fourth Sunday arrived and it was important for me to explain the problem of the bell to them. In the end I had hoped to ask if a single sugar bell would be alright instead of the desired two.

However, Margaret and her husband, Bob, did not attend the service that night.

I was stumped, as the saying goes. What would I do? It was – and still is – my practice to deliver an order *exactly* the way it was requested, not missing a flower, ribbon, or bell. So should I make the decision to present a cake with only one bell? Would they be upset or disappointed with the final result? *Why* oh why wouldn't the partner-bell co-operate!

Another fortnight came and went without being able to catch up with them. I would have only one week remaining to get it right. On that last Sunday evening at church, I saw Bob sitting in the front row as the service began, so I waited until it closed to approach him.

"Hi, how are you?" I asked him, very relieved. "Where is your wife? Is she sick? I wanted to tell her about the problem I'm having with one of the sugar bells – it keeps collapsing on me. Every time it breaks, I re-do it and it collapses again. I don't know what to do with it."

"I'm okay, now," he said pleasantly. "And don't worry about the bell, you see, my wife passed away three weeks ago, about the time you started having problems with your bells. She had a sweet tooth and loved to eat sugar, so it is probably her trying to eat them."

I felt awful and embarrassed that I'd just blurted out my problem without thinking properly. "I'm sorry," I replied. "I hadn't heard about your wife's passing. And I won't go ahead with finishing your cake."

"Oh please, finish it for her sake!" he insisted with a smile. "For I know she would want you to go ahead with it still."

"Then if she is trying to eat them and she really wants me to finish it," I said, making light of the mood, "she had better leave them alone and let me get on with it, so I can bring it along to you next week!"

He gave a little chuckle and said, "that's telling her." Then, addressing the unseen realms he added, "Did you hear her, Dear? Now let her finish the cake so we can eat it together."

We parted company. I went home feeling a little funny at the notion of a sweet-toothed spirit meddling in the creative development of her cherished cake. It was also very sad he'd lost his life-partner after so many years of marriage and so close to their sixtieth anniversary.

The very next morning I tackled the vexing issue of the bell, hoping this one would hold and that Margaret would contain her tempting tastes.

The mixture filled the mould nicely, then detached easily from the cast and held together as it was hollowed out. I then fixed it onto the cake beside its partner bell. On working the final touch-ups in detail I smiled.

"Thank you, Margaret," I said, pleased with how smoothly I was allowed to complete it.

I'm sure I heard a slight voice say, *that's okay, it looks great.*

Bob was delighted when I handed him the cake on the following Sunday at church.

"She would've been very happy with it," he said, admiring the decorative arrangement. "I will have it tomorrow with our family and," he said, pointing to the bells, "I will save the sugar bell for Margaret to eat – if it is possible . . ." and he winked knowingly.

I can very well believe that as soon as she was given 'permission' from him, Margaret would have helped herself with much enthusiasm.

The anniversary cake with sugar bells made for the elderly couple at church

The Man in the Doorway

A month later I was asked by a friend to go to a private home for another group reading. I agreed, though I knew it would be a long night all the same. The booking was for six to eight people, but on arriving, ten people had turned up, all wanting my psychic service. Considering that most sessions lasted for up to an hour per person, this was going to be a *very* long night and I told myself I would need to keep them short! Unfortunately it does not always happen that way, not when there are spirits wanting to talk through you to their loved ones.

Going into my fourth client's session with Carol, I noticed a man appear in the hall doorway behind her, clutching his chest and I gained the sense of six months being connected with him.

"I don't wish to upset you," I said to her, "but have you lost your husband within the last six months?"

"Yes, why do you ask? Does it tell you that in the cards?"

"Yes," I answered, since there was indeed the card which showed that a male had passed in that time, too. "And did he die from a heart attack?"

Amazement overcame her. "Yes, you are spot on!" she said.

"And did he die in a hallway or a corridor?" I asked carefully, wanting to respect her feelings, however I needed to know.

Carol fell quiet, her smile faded and she looked towards the hall door where the man was standing, still holding his chest. Then she looked back at me and quietly said, "Yes, can you see that in the cards too?"

"No," I replied and started to point to him. "He is standing in the doorway over there, clutching his chest.

She gasped. "That's where he died! Right there in our hall!"

This was when I realised Carol was the hostess of the evening and that this was her home; no one had pointed this out to me earlier.

"He's telling me to tell you not to worry about him," I went on. "He's fine now and says that everything is okay." He's saying to me, "Give her all my love. Tell her I'll always be with her, especially when she's feeling down and depressed." He wants you to think of him and he'll help you to feel better."

"Thank you," she replied, with tears brimming. "Thank you so much. I feel better already."

The evening proved to be as busy as anticipated and I managed to get home at around two in the morning, a feat in itself and not something I would care to repeat today.

&⍟&

The Telephone Call

It was a month later when I received an unusual telephone call from a lady trying to sell me some insurance. Of course, I wasn't interested but she persisted in trying to talk me into buying their policy. After letting her speak for some five minutes, I was getting fed up and was about to end the conversation, when I received a clear picture in my head of this lady sitting behind a desk with a high bench-top and a very tall man standing in front of her. It was then I felt the urge to mention this to her, so I did.

"Excuse me for interrupting you, but are you sitting down at a desk with a high bench in front of you?"

She went very quiet for a few minutes, perhaps a touch too long to think about answering.

"Yes, I do, why are you interested?" she finally replied.

I had to think about my own answer, since I didn't want to scare her.

"Do you have a grandfather that has passed over in the last two years?"

Again, silence.

"Why do you want to know?" she asked, with frustration clearly in her voice. I knew she was worried, too, yet I had to get through to her that I could've cared less for her insurance deals and more importantly, that her grandfather was interested in letting her know he was around. I sensed she wanted to know more but was scared to ask for fear I was prying into her private life. Who was I to talk of family members I'd never met? Mind you, this is around the time when I started to get really strong in my medium abilities and though still relatively new at connecting with spirits, let alone asking total strangers about them, I persevered.

"Can you smell roses around you?" for I could see the man handing her a lovely bunch of deep red roses over the bench.

I swear minutes seemed to go on forever waiting for her reply.

"As a matter of fact, I can. How did you know that?"

I then went in with all I had, not to frighten her, but to make her realise she was not alone.

"Well, I am a clairvoyant. I see people and there's a man standing in front of you."

I heard her chuckle of confidence at the other end.

"Sorry, you're wrong there." Evidently she saw nobody in the same room as her. "There's no one here."

"Did you hear what I just said? I'm a clairvoyant," I insisted, feeling quite chuffed that it was now *I* who was asking the questions instead of listening to the rehearsed sale's speech for why I needed their insurance. In fact, I think I was more chuffed at the thought of her talking with the boss later, when he would be asking her if she'd made the sale because it was one deal that had not gone as anticipated.

"I see people," I went on uninterrupted, "and I can see a man who is very tall, quite stocky and he is leaning with his arms resting on the bench top. He is smiling at you. He is also giving you a bunch of red roses with some Babies Breath through them and I feel he was your grandfather. Does this description sound like him?"

Her discomfort dropped on her again, for silence hung on the end of the line. I swear I could hear her thinking, *Oh God, who is this woman?*

Rather shakily, her voice replied, "Yes . . ."

"Well, he wants you to know he is with you," I went on confidently, "to let you realise you are never alone as he is always with you and he's giving you the roses to send you his love. I feel you were very close to him."

"Ahh, yes . . . thank you very much . . . ," she said very softly, clearly with mixed feelings. "Err, thank you, for that . . . I ahh . . ." Another moment on and she picked up pace rather quickly. "I've got more work to go . . . I'd better get back to it." Next thing the call went dead quiet, so to speak. The silence at the other end was not of a confident sales woman shaken to the bone but the dull tone of a caller having hung up the telephone.

I know she was thinking about what I'd said. I know that right then and there her failed attempt to sign me into an insurance deal was *not* her main interest. I never heard from her again and that's okay, at least she got the chance to reconsider her relationship with her grandfather – that he was still around her despite the lack of his physical body. Maybe she thought of him again the next time she smelt roses.

Better yet, she thanked him for his loving gift and smiling, went through the day happy that he is well and watching over her.

৪৩০৪৩

Chapter Five

THE SPIRITUALIST
CHURCH

Manifesting a Lie

At the end of meditation a few weeks later, in one of the weekly open circles at the Church, a man we shall call Mike told us he would go into a trance for us and that he was [quote] "going to manifest himself into some weird being". I recommend, dear reader, that if someone tells you they will do this, take it with an extremely large dose of salt and walk away.

He went through the motions of becoming very still while seated in his chair, his hands clasped between his knees, I guess as though he was already channelling the 'entity'. Presently the twitching started, then he sat up straight and in a strenuous, deep voice, he said, "Hello . . . can you see me?"

"No," many of us replied; could we see what? A man looking no different to a moment ago?

He took to rocking back and forth and he appeared to be experiencing a physical strain of sorts.

"Can you see me now?" he repeated, in a slightly raised but growling voice.

"No," we replied. Should we have?

Apparently this made him quite angry, presumably because the 'something weird' hadn't shown itself. He was going through his motions again – which included more growling – when I started to smell this musty waft of moth balls.

I realised at this point that I had a spirit standing immediately to my left. At first I recognised the feet, clad in golden sandals, then higher up, the white robes fastened in place with golden cord and gold trimmings on the hemline. The heavenly man once seen in my Mum's bedroom all of those years ago at the tender age of eleven had returned.

Mike, meanwhile, was almost red in the face from trying so hard to manifest his weird being.

"Can you see me *now*?" he screamed.

A couple of people said "yes", though I think they were scared that Mike was about to go mad and attack someone if he got the undesired 'no' again. It was a charade, I knew this and more so because my god-like figure beside me was quite incensed.

"He lies! He lies!" he said to me. "*Tell them he lies!*"

I was sure the other people in the circle could hear him, too. But no one flinched and Mike was doing his level best at trying to prove he was something that he wasn't, so perhaps they doubted hearing my spirit's angry voice.

Calmly I spoke to my angel. *'I can't tell them he's lying. They won't believe me.'*

His otherworldly presence started to rise up off the floor; he was ropable and I could feel it.

"He lies! *He lies!*" he insisted over and over. "*Tell them* he lies!"

'I can't,' I mentally replied again, *'If I say that, they may think I'm jealous that I'm not like him and may want me to prove it. Besides, even if he is lying, what harm is he doing? He is only play-acting. You and I know he is lying, but so what? Let him have his fun. If I were to tell them he was lying because I heard you telling me so, they may think that* I'm *lying.'*

You must understand that for me, this was still at a time when I was finding my way in the field of psychic and spiritual development – I was still too new to a thing called channelling, for example. I was not necessarily a confident person to begin with, nor someone who knew how to confront another with real authority, so the thought of pulling into line an assumed professional in his element was well beyond my expertise. My angel-figure must have taken this into account.

"Oh, alright!" he grumbled, while levitating in the air. "But he displeases me deeply! Do what you think is best."

'Thank you,' I answered, relieved.

He faded away, smell and all.

Mike carried along playing the part of a Weird Being and we, his audience, sat there watching him rather like idiots until finally the show was over. I'd like to think he was in the running for Worst Channeller of the Year Award, but I doubted he had many followers – well, I hoped he didn't.

What I drew from this evening, however, was knowing inwardly that I had been communicating with a much higher spirit – one who *did* carry authority. Who could say if it was God or Jesus, or my guardian angel? I cannot be certain even to this day, though I expect I will find out when it is my time to go over to their side. It was wonderful to be in company with a remembered face, for it tells me that he was always there with me, even though I couldn't see him.

This is how it is with Spirit. We go from day to day and moment to moment so absorbed in what we do; slaving in the workplace, raising the kids, watching television, eating and drinking with friends, burying a loved one. The list is endless and our minds habitually keep us 'stuck' in that level of consciousness, hardly letting us 'surface' to the higher awareness where our souls exist. It is a matter of knowing only what we can see and hear, touch, taste or smell at the time, or of listening to the fancies of our imagination as it pulls us between past events and future wants.

Only with constant practice at attuning our minds to the non-physical dimension of Spirit do we begin to notice an 'other' existence. We must start with catching ourselves at every possible chance if only to remind us that "Mother is there", or "My father said he'll always be with me, even if I can't see him". Those fleeting lights you might glimpse in your peripheral view is often that someone in spirit watching over you. The strange noise down the hall, in the next room, upstairs, or downstairs or from wherever nearby that you *know* wasn't made by the pet or fellow house-mate, will typically be a means of someone deceased telling you of their presence.

They are *always* with us. They want to be with us, just as much as we want them to be with us. Life doesn't stop because the body has ended. Intelligence is what got us here in the first place, it is what created this whole thing we call the universe, the Big Bang and the Armageddon (which is an end of an era, or a culture, or a way of living, a belief system. It is not the complete destruction of all of life in one hit).

Before I left that night for home, Mike came up to me and said the most oddest thing; "You're gonna be zapped next week."

I shuddered, wondering what he meant by 'zapped'.

"What, not me?" I replied, trying to deflect the comment.

"Yep. You'll be zapped, you'll see."

ℂ℃℄

My wonderful husband came with me the following week, because it worried me what Mike had said and I wanted a bit of 'back up' in case any shenanigans had been planned. People like Mike are inclined to take you for a ride and particularly in today's climate, they may try advances that they are well and truly unentitled to.

We formed our circle and entered meditation as usual and after a little while I heard an elderly woman who I think may have been co-running the circle speak.

"I think she's ready," she whispered to somebody whom I didn't see (my eyes were closed and my head was lowered).

It sounded as if she was right behind me, but it couldn't have been so. *It's not me*, I thought, *it must be another lady near me*'. All of a sudden I felt a hand on my right shoulder.

"Are you all right?" she whispered in my ear.

I went cold. *What do I do now? This is silly! Of course I'm o.k.* I had been taught that while in meditation, you are to block out the sounds around you, as well, you should not come out of a deep meditation too quickly. You can be left 'in limbo' if this happens, apparently.

I focused on remaining calm, told myself I was dreaming and that nothing untoward was happening to me. *Just relax*, I said internally and hoped we would hear someone else speak up.

But then, both my shoulders were held beneath a pair of hands and she whispered to me again.

"Is there anybody with us?"

I froze. I sensed an uncanny presence around me, as though I was trapped in someone else's body.

"What is your name?" the woman asked softly.

I couldn't answer her, yet I must have said something because the next thing I knew, she was asking me another question.

"Where are you?" she said. "Can you describe your surroundings?"

In that strange mode of detachment, (where you seem not to be in your body but you know it is responding), I recall talking to her. I remember trying to tell her I was okay, but the words wouldn't come out. It was as if I stood in the background, watching a movie of myself in action and this is when I understood I was channelling a spirit. Was I in her body, or was she in mine? I couldn't tell.

"I am in a concrete shelter," I replied, though I knew it wasn't really me saying the words. "It is dark and it has no windows, only a door."

"Stand up Love, and walk towards the door," she gently said. "Go outside."

Yet I couldn't move. My legs felt paralysed and, as dreams will go, I became aware that I was crippled and in a wheelchair. I started to cry and explained this to her.

Calmly, almost tenderly, the lady's voice continued to whisper close in my ear.

"Don't be afraid, dear. Just try to stand up and if you start to fall, we'll be here to help you up again. You are okay now. You're in good hands, trust me."

I remember standing up although in reality, I could tell that my body had stayed seated; it was a weird feeling. The lady held on to my arms and encouraged me to approach the door and go outside. A tingling feeling went through my limbs as I started to walk, the same effect one gets with a lack of blood circulation, I think and I was incredibly weak from prolonged inactivity. Finally I reached the door and on opening it, bright, bright sunlight awaited.

The light was warm and intense and presently I saw a path leading away to somewhere, lined on both sides with masses of multicoloured tulips. The beauty and perfume of the flowers were stunning.

"Can you see anyone you might know?" the lady asked.

The voice inside of me replied. "No."

"Walk down the pathway until you can see someone," she urged.

So I walked to the end of this path where a big tree – reminiscent of a Liquid Amber – spread its branches. A man stood beneath, with his hand stretched forth to me, gently beckoning for me to go to him.

"I can see a man standing under a big tree," I explained.

"Go to him," she said, "and he will help you to go into the light."

Closer to him I realised I had seen him before, when I was a child, only he didn't have his crown on yet he was dressed in his white and gold robes. Comfortable that I was indeed safe and well, I accepted his hand.

The contact brought a jolt within me, forcing me out of my dreamy condition and I found myself 'back' in the church hall, halfway across the circle. I very nearly fell down, though the elderly lady and another man had been waiting there with me, catching me by the elbows and helping me to steady myself.

I regained my composure and looked around at the stunned faces of the circle: even my husband held a perplexed expression, as though he couldn't believe what he had just witnessed. A couple of people said I had looked different while in this trance-like state, as though my appearance had changed slightly, though I was oblivious of it. I have since learnt that when a person channels a spirit, facial distortions can occur, as well as the more commonly experienced voice-alteration, posture and mannerisms.

About all I knew was how warm and funny I felt all over and at how uplifting the encounter was. The lady explained to me that what had transpired was called Rescue Work, in which the 'trapped spirit' is coaxed out of their confined situation and encouraged to 'cross over' to a peaceful after-life. In this case, the spirit I had unwittingly helped was caught in the belief that she was forever disabled and the dark room became a visual representation of such lasting confinement. How she and I connected is a mystery for me, though it was obviously clear to me that without the whispering words of encouragement, she'd not have realised her mind-set had been controlling her beyond death. Chances are she was unaware of having died physically and quite possibly thought she was in a long, on-going dream.

I am happy for her that I helped to cross her over and accepted her as another of my spirit friends. It was after enjoying my cuppa later that night that I reckoned I knew now what Mike had meant by being 'zapped'.

ꚉꚑ

Trudy's Ordeal

In today's open-minded climate, where people talk readily of Reiki, crystal healing, astral travelling or the like, society, on the whole, accepts it. Sure there are still plenty of people who write off the paranormal as baloney, but there are many, many others more willing to consider possibilities beyond the known facts and we are much nearer now to the place where science is discovering truths in metaphysics. Among them, psychic communication, which through means of sensitive mechanics, has proven that everyone's thoughts can be seen in the form of electromagnetic wavelengths.

I am no expert on how scientists have achieved this, the point is, our thoughts *do* exist beyond the brain and though our mortal eyes don't see them, they are there all the same, transmitting what we think into the atmosphere around us. Think of a light bulb; we flick a switch on the wall and invisible currents of electricity travel through wires to the bulb – the light comes on in the lamp as an *external* result of the intention.

Similarly, what is 'drifting about' in that space around us can be picked up in our minds. In this case, consider your television or radio at work, in which the visual and audio output comes to us from the electronically transmitted wavelengths it *receives* on the air from the station. These are very simplified illustrations here, but the principle is the same: we don't *see* the movie coming to our television, or the D.J.'s voice on the radio, but we can still *see* or *hear* the movie or voice as it moves through the 'brain' of mechanics in the television or radio.

You get the idea. Psychic people and mediums have merely sharpened the wiring in their minds to allow them better reception of the thought transmissions constantly surrounding us all. Everyone of us has the mental nuts and bolts to pick up on these high vibrational wavelengths, we just need to realise that we also have the ability to re-tune the box in order to get clarity of the psychic images and communication. For some of us, we are blessed with a perfectly working receiver from birth or childhood. For many more of us, we have to work at it.

At one of our open circles a few weeks following the trapped spirit's crossing over, the teacher of our meditation circle asked us to try sharing in a 'group clairvoyance'. This was inspired by recent news events of missing people and he hoped that by all of us focusing on a specific event or person, we might be able to gain insights that the police had not. With more than one mind concentrating, we would have a greater chance of picking up multiple clues than say, one individual.

It was important that we were all willing to try this and equally important that we could be open-minded to the idea of it working, for where there is doubt (specifically where even one of us might be cynical), the flow of these higher vibrations may be stymied, lost, or even distorted. This can be a frequent experience when a sitter waits for you to read their cards but all you can see is pictures without interpretation, or, as with the angry spirit of Mafia description, the cards go blank.

Of course we were all willing to attempt something which could help bring peace to grieving and frustrated families of the missing. Unfortunately, very little came through and though a few of us felt something, nothing of reasonable information could be distinguished.

"Trudy is here," was all one lady said and another had agreed that she had heard the same name. I, too, very clearly heard this name. Someone else reported the word 'Fugy', another, 'Bluey' and someone else thought they heard 'Suzy'. Obviously we were sensing the same sound of pronunciation and difficulty in accuracy can be as much a part of the training psychic as it can be for the communicating spirit, (they, too, are re-learning how to send us their thoughts).

We neither recognised the name nor knew what it might stand for, so we dismissed it in deep frustration, closed the meditation and eventually went home. The lack of results may not have been due to sceptical participants on this occasion, as nearly everyone of us were beginners and the aim of the experience was simply to 'try', in which feedback amongst us would serve as confirmation, i.e. more than one person independently receiving the name Trudy.

I was unhappy that night because I felt I had let the spirit down and no doubt others in the circle had felt similar. I never found out if any of them had ever received further communication from 'Trudy', but it seemed my heart had not let go. It was the very next day when the children had gone to school and I had picked up my tools to make icing flowers for a birthday cake when she returned. I had started to relax while forming the first petal of the flower.

'*Trudy is here,*' a female spirit said very softly.

'*What do you mean? And how can I help you?*' I asked, uncertain with the statement.

'*Tell my family I am here,*' she said.

I decided to put the icing down and concentrate on the spirit's plea, for there was urgency in her tone. I needed to have peace and quiet to hear her and just as I went to turn off the radio so I could tune into her mental vibrations, the news came on.

"There is still no word on the young hitchhiker who went missing last night," the announcer said. "Trudy was last seen on the North Shore. If anyone can help the police with her whereabouts, please contact the North Shore police station."

It really did happen just like that. I went cold. I turned off the radio and immediately began to meditate. The strong feeling of a lady's presence came to me and I asked her if this was the spirit of the missing hitchhiker, or was I just imagining it.

Using mental imagery – or picture form – she showed me what had happened to her;

She was hitchhiking on the main road when a white or creamy van pulled over and a youngish man, probably around early to mid twenties, indicated for her to get in. As she relaxed in his company, I sensed another man also in the van with them, but never actually saw him. I sensed he was hiding in the back.

"What's your name?" the driver asked her.

"Trudy," she replied.

I shuddered, for it was the same name I'd heard only the night before – around the time of the hitchhiker's disappearance. Nausea came over me.

The man drove down the road and I began to feel danger around her.

'*What is his name?*' I asked her, but at this point she was in trouble. As though I was seeing things from her perspective, I could feel myself being pushed down to the floor of the van, possibly by the figure in the back.

She pointed to a street sign and I looked up in time to clearly read the words 'John Fitzgerald'. I took this to be the driver's name. I knew by now that I had to be tuned in to her spirit vibrations, when I saw him turning into a darkened street. There was a struggle and then he hit her. She fought to get up. A hand grabbed me around my neck and I was being strangled and I was being held down by who I think was the other man.

The scene went dark momentarily and then the driver continued to take the van to the corner of Albert Street, Palm Beach. I felt that at this stage she was gone I heard the driver calling out "Brian what have you done, – she was now dead. Outside of the vehicle where they'd stopped was a thick stand of black bushes, a bit like mulberry, blueberry, or possibly raspberry. What struck me most was how prickly the bushes were and they had little berries on them. I saw someone pick up her body and throw it into them, where they left her.

I was in tears at the tragic way she had been killed and so very frightened that it was true. I searched the phone book for the Palm Beach police station, told them my name and what I had seen and how I had heard her name in the circle only the night before. I went on to describe how Trudy's spirit had come to me the next morning and how she had shown me in detail what had transpired with the two men. I urged them to please investigate the area for her remains.

Sadly, given the stifled attitudes of the day, the policeman on the other end of the phone just laughed it off.

"Sure Love, we'll check it out," he said, but I could tell by his voice that he didn't believe me.

I was furious. I did not make calls like this for the fun of it. In fact I was quite intimidated to express the sort of psychic communications I had with just anyone, let alone simply making a prank call to the local police shop! How dare that fellow – someone who has sworn to protect the community – right me off as a nutcase!

"I'm sorry, Trudy," I said to her. "I have done my best but I'm sure they don't believe me. I am truly sorry."

I believe she understood my dilemma and though looking very sad, she vanished and has not, to my knowledge, returned. I wanted to cry so hard for her; she had been robbed of a life and had had no opportunity to speak to her loved ones before leaving them. I prayed for her and cried for a long, long time afterwards and I had hoped the perpetrators would be caught and jailed for their crime. I wanted them to suffer worse than what she had suffered.

To this day it haunts me. I have never heard anything more about the case; there is no closure and for Trudy, perhaps no proper burial. I can only hope that a psychic or medium so much stronger than I had been able to convince the detectives to re-open the case. It has been over thirty years now and I have heard many times of how bodies are found well after their deaths and through modern forensic techniques, their identities can be established, sometimes even leading to the perpetrators, who may still receive sentencing for their crimes.

I can only hope Trudy forgave me for not pushing the police any further back then and that she has since found peace in the face of this horrible crime.

৪০৪

The Closed Circle

Some two months later a medium from the spiritualist church invited me to attend a closed circle that she regularly went to,. Initially I was hesitant, not knowing what would be expected of me, but I soon learned there was little difference between the open one at the church and a closed circle in the privacy of one's home.

Primarily, a closed circle has usually only a few participants who have been invited into it, (on group consensus) and for it to be a strong unit, they each must attend every session. A target activity is pre-chosen for all to concentrate their various skills on and it is important that harmony resides between individuals, that respect of each other and for the practice is acknowledged, because the experiences you have can be highly personal. As well, those in spirit come to know the strengths of the members, they have the chance to establish 'routine' based on the stability of the group and therefore channel their own energies on a more concentrated level. Some terrific achievements can develop from closed circles, as I had found out.

By comparison, an open circle allows for a variety of 'visitors', in which no two faces may be the same from week to week and it is not uncommon for there to be quite a number people involved. The upside of this is that, should personal issues arise, such as needy children or health concerns, you have no obligation to turn up at the next session. Learning can still be achieved though perhaps at a slower rate.

Being asked into this closed gathering by Peggy brought me a sense of acceptance – I was honoured to be counted as an equal among my peers. The best part was that I could still attend the open circle if I wanted to. The learning I gained from this group was very rewarding for my future psychic development, in which I not only saw spirits, but heard them guiding me in my daily life as well.

It felt like a second family coming together. I grew stronger and stronger, I was on a higher plane and so were the others. We lasted about three years until it folded due to the host's wife taking ill, in which Peggy offered to hold it at her place. During each weekly session I would receive messages for the others and was able to give them advice or direction of how to help themselves in understanding my visions. Peggy could channel (properly) and she always talked to us through her guides with important answers to our questions.

We lasted for a further three and a half years when sadly, I had to leave them, for my family had agreed to move to Western Australia; a trip I would come to regret.

ঙ০৫৪

PART TWO

THE CHANGE OF
A LIFETIME

Chapter Six

SPIRITUALLY LOST

A Devastating Request

We sold our home in the hills district of outer Sydney in 1984 and temporarily moved our family of six with our caravan to my oldest sister's driveway in Lethbridge Park. We needed time to sort out which route across the country we would take to our final destination, however in the last week before actually leaving our house, when the younger children were still at school and my husband at work, my oldest son, Arthur, asked me a question that floored me.

"Mum, would you do Dad and me a favour?" he calmly said.

"If I can," I replied hesitatingly, not liking the tone in his words.

"Will you . . ." he began with a quiver in his voice, "stop what you are doing?"

"That's a strange request. What do you mean by that?"

"When we get settled in W.A., will you please not talk to spirits and stop reading people's cards?"

I felt like he'd just ripped my heart out. Having the gift was something I had wanted for so long and I had studied very hard to learn it. this was a part of my body, that's how important it was to me.

"Why are you asking me to give my beautiful gift away that I treasure so much?" I asked.

"It upsets Dad and me and the family," he replied. "We don't like strangers coming into our home to see ghosts and we feel that it is evil." He was so physically close to me that he may as well have been holding my hand; he was trying to be so discreet about it, that he was almost whispering.

I suspect 'Dad' was the excuse, for my husband had very rarely said anything negative when it came to the spirit work or my interest in the subject. He only stepped in once or twice when the situation became questionable to my safety. What was I to say? What do I do?

"I want us to make a fresh start, Mum," he went on and his beautiful brown eyes pleaded in silence.

This was all very disappointing for me because I truly thought they didn't mind. But obviously I was wrong. I loved my son, my husband and my family and their happiness had to come first. The hardest thing for me to do would come within the hour.

Before I continue this account, I must include a relevant story which should help to illustrate young Arthur's perspective, for it was because of this which brought me to this pivotal – almost irreversible – act.

The shift to my sister's home was a very difficult time, for both families had young teens now and for up to a couple of years previous, Arthur had secretly been suffering mental health problems for which we, as his parents, were unaware of. He had experienced a turbulent birth and childhood, with more than one head injury incurred and I don't know, but perhaps it was through these circumstances which lead him to finding comfort in Sunday school, joining up with the local youth group and regularly going to Christian church services, (who deny psychic work as the Devil's practice).

Either way, his exposure to religious attitudes compromised the path I was on with my own beliefs and I can only say on reflection that he had become brainwashed with Christian ideals by the time we were moving. My poor baby, he had obviously been so affected that, when asked to call into a friend's house to pick up a certain book for me (it was on the route home and therefore not a special trip to take), he did, had obviously glanced through it and decided he would be 'saving me' from such deception and evil that he disposed of it at the shopping centre bin.

The book, of course, was all about spiritual matters, a metaphysical book for which I had hoped to gain more insight into a subject I loved. Needless to say, when he braved the fierce presence of his parents that afternoon – and it must've taken a huge amount of courage, for I was livid – he copped the brunt of severe punishment. Bravely he told us how 'wrong' spiritual activities really were, of how God disapproved and that all good Christians should also disapprove. I didn't hold this religious belief, especially when I'd always asked God to protect me.

It was a confronting experience, to say the least, to have your beloved child tell you how unhappy and disappointed they were with you when all along you were oblivious to their feelings of it. I understand now that we had no idea what he was going through, on the whole and in the meantime we were trying to marshal our belongings for a journey more than two-thousand miles away.

&⁊Cℜ

And so, on the afternoon of his devastating request, with a heart sunken beyond the depths of my soul, I prayed to all my spirit friends to forgive me for what I was about to ask of them. I thanked my guides for my precious gift of spirit communication that I had longed for. I dearly hoped they would understand the loyalty I held to my family and that my request for them to leave me would be respected.

I prayed to God Almighty that when the time was right for me, could I please receive my gift back, for I did not, in truth, wish to lose it entirely. Then I applied the visualising techniques of deep meditation; I imagined a very fine white curtain at each side of a large stage, where all of my spirit friends stood and with tears in my eyes, I did the hardest thing in my life at the time – I said goodbye.

To all of them I gave my farewell, desperate in the hopes they understood me, that I needed to keep peace within my family. I told them how much I loved them, that I would miss them terribly and that hopefully one day I would get my gift back and meet up with them all again. Then I imagined the curtain closing, covering those beautiful faces, hiding their loving warmth from me. It was devastating, for these people were as real to me as any in the physical world and they had been with me through many experiences, always gentle, always there. And here was I turning my back on them.

Once the curtain had closed I felt desolately empty and horribly alone.

Afterwards I told Arthur it was all over and I wouldn't do it anymore.

He smiled, relieved, thoroughly innocent to the ache inside of me. I hurt so badly within that I didn't know how I would get through the coming days, weeks, months, or years. All that went over and over in my mind was, *what have I done?*

It was going to be a big lesson for me in time, a thing which would culminate in me writing this book. Nevertheless, I yearned to understand why this had to have happened to me, after trying so hard to make the spirit connections that could and would help those in need of guidance.

I say again, nothing happens by chance . . . there is a reason for everything.

&⁊Cℜ

The Long Journey West

In three vehicles we travelled across Australia, spending a day on the road and a day resting in a major town. There were many interesting places and we maintained frequent contact with relatives in the east so they knew where we were on any given day. At Ceduna in South Australia we were forced to stay for up to three days due to a brake-down in our son's car and which needed parts delivered in to get us back on the road.

My husband's parents', now elderly and frail in health and who had been unhappy to see us leave, were dismayed with the phone call from Ceduna, as they didn't think we were serious about going that far away. In hindsight, the realisation must have been a blow to them.

Between the mini convoy in which I, my husband and Arthur drove, with siblings Debbie, Kevin, Christine, four dogs and two rosella's as our passengers, contact was via C.B. radio. There are only two major highways to the city of Perth once you reach Norseman in W.A.; one which takes the road-traveller north to Kalgoorlie and one that leads in the opposite direction to Esperance. At Balladonia, (well passed the state border), we rang my oldest sister to let her know we were safe and stopping there for the night and that we would be driving north to Kalgoorlie the next day.

The curious ways of Spirit will play it's part irrelevant of one's standpoint on their presence, or presumed omission of it. The next day's plans changed when we passed through Norseman around lunch time, for on consulting the map as we filled the cars with petrol, we decided to head south to Esperance.

I had one of those weird feelings as had occurred back in Sydney with Arthur's request and here was I on the other side of the country only a week later, with no spirit communication, just getting used to the idea of being 'on my own', with no one to guide me of any direction. I was running on intuition, I suppose you could say.

Some six hours down the road I was thinking that it was getting late and we needed to find a town to sleep in soon. We were not able to get reception on the radio on this journey and were also in favour of keeping the airwaves relatively clear of noise should we need to hear contact from another on the C.B. Perhaps Clive and Arthur played cassettes, but I preferred the silence. For some reason I decided to turn on the radio, just in case some sort of music was to come on and it would help to break the boredom of distance, then maybe it was someone in the spirit world trying to warn me of what was to come. To my amazement this was the first thing I heard:

"– Stay tuned for the seven o'clock news coming up next, as we have a special police announcement," a lady said.

I was rather excited to be receiving something in the middle of nowhere, so I called through to my husband and son on the C.B. to ask if they'd had their car radios on.

"No, why?" came their answers.

So I relayed the message from the announcer, so they agreed to tune in as well. A moment later her voice came over the airwaves.

"*. . . Good evening. We have a very important police message to anyone knowing the whereabouts of the Duncan family, travelling from the Eastern States and currently in the Kalgoorlie area of Western Australia. Could you please contact the Kalgoorlie police urgently with any information . . .*"

We were stunned. A shiver went down my spine as I wondered what was so urgent that we had to contact the police, knowing that for more than half of our journey so far, I had not even slightly considered turning the radio on. Therefore, we would not have heard the news.

As 'luck' was on our side, we had only travelled a further ten minutes when we saw a sign saying, *Salmon Gums*. A short drive on and we came across a little shop with an old red telephone box out on the front footpath and behind the shop was a small caravan park. My husband made the call to the Kalgoorlie police, who were amazed we had responded so quickly, as the bulletin had been the first report aired. They didn't expect us to get the message for a couple of hours because we were on the move over such a large area and even more surprised when they'd learned my husband was calling from the southern route.

"We are sorry to have some bad news for you, Mr. Duncan," they said. "Your father has passed away earlier today."

It turned out my husband's mother didn't know how to get in touch with us and had phoned my older sister to see if she knew where we were. As we'd told my sister of our plans to go north, she assumed the best thing was to contact the Kalgoorlie police and hope they would find us. I could not shake thoughts about the continued presence of Spirit and my question was, are my angels looking after me, or was it God's way of telling me he was still with me?

All I knew was we were blessed that day, even though the news was tragic. It could have been worse, we may not have heard the news until the next day, or at all. It certainly would not have occurred until we'd next rang a relative for an update of our location and well-being. We spent the night at the caravan park behind the shop and hurried for Esperance the very next day, in the hopes my husband could catch a plane to Sydney.

Unknown to us, Esperance did not have an airport, not even a light aircraft service that could connect with Perth, so instead of our intended scenic journey towards this city, we chose to fuel up our vehicles here and continue on to Perth the next day. It would so happen that this was a long weekend and all petrol stations in the area were closed until the following Tuesday (these in an era before seven-day-week trading).

Of course the delays tormented us, yet we just had to wait it out. Later, we suspected the series of circumstances were perhaps Spirit's way of holding us back from erroneously speeding through a full-day's journey, for which we would probably have been driver-fatigued by nightfall and on the wrong side of an accident. The three day interval allowed us the necessary chance to collect ourselves, to relax and take in some sights of the region, so by the time Tuesday morning arrived, we were refreshed and more importantly, calm behind the wheel.

Relevant calls were made to both my sister and mother-in-law each night to explain our plan to send my husband back to them by week's end. Through it all I could sense a spiritual someone with me, telling me not to worry, but I couldn't say who it was since I had told them to 'go away'. So I put my trust in God's hand that it would all work out well, we filled up with petrol and headed off.

On dusk, nineteen days after leaving Sydney, we pulled in to a caravan park on the outskirts of Perth. The owners were wonderful. When we explained to them of our situation, they urged us to settle in and not worry, for they would look after us for however long my husband needed while away in Sydney. After a quick meal we drove to the airport, intending to book the very next flight out for him, but the rules of the day there were rather strange, because tickets were required for booking a minimum of four days in advance, otherwise one had to wait in line for the a 'twenty-four-hour standby' flight.

We explained the urgency of our predicament, pleading with airline staff to make an exception to the rules. Someone must have felt sorry for us, I suppose, for eventually a supervisor was brought in to assist us and before long, a flight leaving for Sydney early the next morning was arranged. Perhaps the supervisor had telephoned the police for verification of the facts? Maybe it was higher intervention that stepped in? Either way, we were so grateful that we didn't ask too many questions, but accepted the ticket and left the airport smiling with joy. My husband returned back to W.A. a week later after comforting his mother and attending his father's funeral.

⅄ⅅ

Three Funerals

Upon his return we found a distant cousin on my husband's side of the family living fifteen minutes drive from the caravan park and after a short visit with her she offered us to stay in her backyard until we could find a nice house to buy. Within the month we had found a new home for our family up in the hills district and yet, sadness was still to come. One week after moving in my oldest sister rang to tell us that her husband, Alan, had passed away suddenly that morning. This would mean another speedy trip back to N.S.W. on short notice – and only four weeks in the wake of my father-in-law's death.

Alan was more than a brother by marriage; he and my husband had spent the greater part of their childhood and young adult lives together, going through school together, even working in the same job at the same workplace. They were best friends as much as brother-in-laws. The blow was like a double whammy and the circumstances under which Alan died have left us all feeling uncomfortable, since the circumstances surrounding his death have not been satisfactorily proven.

Three months prior to his death, through no fault of his own, Alan was severely beaten by a neighbourhood bully. The bashing was brutal – kicks to his stomach and chest caused blood clots and one of these are believed to have blocked the heart valve. Although clinical results stated he'd suffered a coronary occlusion, a medical expert at the time indicated the head trauma he'd suffered did lead to the heart condition that eventuated.

On settling into our new area, we kept in contact with the distant cousin who lived nearby and told her of our ordeal. She offered us her help, so we left our children and pets in her care for the couple of weeks of our return to N.S.W. by coach. Although I had told my spirit friends to go away only a month or two prior, it soon became obvious that Alan was unaware I did not want to communicate with those in spirit (then again, he could also be a stubborn man). While at the funeral, standing at the back of the hearse next to the coffin, with Hilda and her youngest daughter not far off, I suddenly heard this almighty scream come from inside of it.

"Hild*aa*!" he yelled, quite distressed. "Hild*aa*! Get me out of here!"

I looked at Hilda's face, realising she could not hear him.

"*Hilda*! help me!"

I was sure somebody would hear him, for his voice was so clear and loud and for all accounts, right there with us. But of course, as it dawned on me, I understood I was the only one who could help him to cross over; he was definitely gone from this earthly plane. Using all of my strengths and mental abilities to call upon my guides, I asked them to help me cross my brother-in-law over. Just as he was starting to call Hilda's name again, I 'spoke' to him.

'*She can't hear you,*' I thought to him, '*but I can.*'

"Hild*aah*!" he insisted. "*Hildaah!*"

'*Alan, can you see a light around you?*'

"Yes," came his reply.

'*You have died and you must go to the Light. Look around your surroundings and see if you can see your Nan. Go to her and she will show you the way through the Light.*'

All went quiet and it would seem he had listened to me, although he may of not crossed over but I hoped at least he was with family members. I thanked my guides and hoped also that he'd gone willingly. Being able to sense my spirits still watching over me was a good feeling and I felt honoured when I'd left the funeral to think I may have positively helped Alan in his moment of need – a task that other's there might well have misunderstood, or have feared if they'd seen or heard him.

Much, much later Hilda told us of an experience she'd had with a clairvoyant because, as she'd said, "It didn't feel right". She meant, of course, Alan's death; she was uneasy regarding the circumstances surrounding it, as well as the results that had come of it. Needing answers, she consulted the clairvoyant ten weeks after his passing and thankfully, Alan's spirit came through.

"He's standing next to you," she said to Hilda.

In the following discussion, an important message revealed the reason why Alan had called out to her at the funeral; he wasn't ready to go. He was sorry about essential papers he hadn't signed – eighteen years of superannuation payments which she could now do with. Hilda had had difficulty settling his affairs and it made sense to hear of his deep concern

My Encounters with the Spirit World

and apology, which he took this meeting to convey, as well. He was also puzzled about the 'disappearance' of other personal effects, including his wristwatch and ties and through the clairvoyant he asked Hilda what she'd done with them.

"I put them in the wardrobe," she said. Evidently Alan didn't know this.

By the end of the session the clairvoyant relayed Alan's parting words to Hilda (kindly repeated here with Hilda's permission):

"He's going now. He's satisfied he has gotten through to you, to tell you how sorry he is – not leaving you with anything, especially any money. He's ready to cross over now."

೮ఆ

Before returning to Western Australia, my husband and I went to visit his mother, not realising that this, too, was to be the last time we'd see her. Three days later we arrived back in W.A. to our new home after a long and wearying coach drive. We were grateful to our second-cousin for minding the children and pets in our absence and then soon began to re-settle into a routine. But in the fourth week back, it happened all over again.

Another dreadful call from family in the east told us of my brother's partner passing away with bone cancer. Unfortunately we'd drained our funds for travelling to the last two funerals, nor did we want to impose on our newly-acquainted second-cousin with caring for our children and pets again. We sent our condolences and love and hoped fervently there would be no more such news for a while to come. In an unfamiliar setting, so far away from family and friends, the trauma of loss or serious health concerns was something we did not want to experience again.

Five months from first leaving N.S.W., when we had finally begun to get on top of it all, the dreaded call came from Clive's brother, Brian – a mere six weeks behind the previous death. For my husband, it was the worst news he could have ever received. His mother had been found slumped in her chair with a cold cup of tea on the table; it was as though she'd gone to sleep and had never woke up.

He was devastated.

"I will get over there as soon as I can," he'd said.

"I'd like you all to come back for the funeral," his brother, Brian, had said.

"We can't," my husband replied, "We can only afford to send me back."

"Sorry," Brian added, "but you are all coming over in two days' time. Just go down to the coach terminal tomorrow and pick up your tickets for everyone, because I've already booked and paid for them."

We were stunned. How do you thank someone for buying six full-fare tickets for a three-day return coach drive across the country? And at short notice? Thankfully the second-cousin agreed to house-sit our pets for the fortnight so I stocked up with pet food for her while we would be away and Nell, though you have since passed on yourself, we are grateful for your understanding and that you were there for us then.

As with Alan's funeral, I sensed spirits comforting me at the service and saw fleeting glimpses of what looked like ghostly figures walking around members of my husband's family. I could not recognise any of them and I expect that this was due to my former request for their absence from my conscious awareness.

⁎⌘⁎

The 'Disturbed' House

Perhaps we may be understood for worrying over the next telephone call that would carry news of another loved-one's death and the concerns we'd have for conveying us to their funerals and back again. Integrating into the new community – it's social and economic environment – proved to be as difficult for each of us as was the trauma of four family deaths in a row. Steady work was hard to find, often it was only on a casual basis and dirty. Sadly we found many West Australian people held a 'them and us' mentality; you're from the Eastern States, you're not local, we don't accept you. It was a rather common, discriminating attitude in those days, which left us feeling further isolated from the mainstream 'Australia'. And then there was our 'disturbed' house . . .

Built in a heavily treed area, with native bush surrounding it and brick paving lining the courtyard veranda on all sides, this was one place that clearly held an active spiritual presence. Strange, unexplainable noises were always being heard. Evidently a ghost-woman enjoyed visiting this house and she wore high heels, for her shoes would come tapping along the bricks to the back door on many occasions.

Once, my youngest daughter, Christine, was in the bathroom when she'd heard the footsteps. The bathroom was separated from the back door only by a small-roomed toilet and she called out to me to let me know we had a visitor. I went to the door expecting to see someone, though no one was there. I checked all of the other doors to the house and even the outside to the driveway and still nobody was seen.

At first we wondered if it was either a neighbourhood prank, or if we'd simply imagined it, but when various members and visitors also heard it over the months we had lived there, it became a frustration. Of course there were times when we really *did* have a high-heeled visitor, who we welcomed in, however, once in a while we had delayed answering the door because we thought the approaching steps were 'the Lady'. But the other cause for frustration, personally speaking, was my inability to see her, or to communicate with her, in which I could've helped her to cross over. I felt helpless and prayed to God to help her. I had truly begun to regret the promise I'd made to my son and husband by this point.

It was not uncommon for us to smell cigarette or cigar smoke in or around the house, though none of my family either smoked then, or today. Perhaps the most frightening aspect of this property was the tree stump in the driveway, which had the lines of a disturbing, evil face in its bark. I cannot pin-point any specific happenings with this trunk, yet the atmosphere around it felt very, very awful.

Whenever I looked at it I felt frightened, as though if I went too closely to it, it would jump out of the ground and grab me. Darkness seemed to emanate from it, while its 'eyes' watched you over the drive and gardens. We all felt it, we were all similarly affected with disharmony whenever we gave it our attention. You may be wondering why we bought the property with it there, but the fact was, none of us had actually noticed it in the beginning, it was as though it had just appeared out of nowhere.

It is interesting to note that the property had had many owners and that for every couple who had lived in it, they had broken up in divorce or endured long-term separation. Even my husband and I were parted from each other for several months while he had temporarily returned to his old Sydney job, for he couldn't find local work in our area. He was either too qualified or not qualified enough but in reality he was classified as an Eastern Stater and there was no room for outsiders. Those months without him were long, difficult and bitter and the strength of our relationship was sorely tested.

Prior to leaving for this job, whilst in our early months at the new house and managing to find casual employment as a labourer, my husband was removing rust from steel frames in the rear yard of an old factory when he heard his mother's voice.

"Oh Clive, you don't have to do this."

He looked around, expecting to see her, but of course she wasn't there. The nature of his work was back-breaking and gritty and not ordinarily his line of profession. Apparently his mum was watching over him, unhappy that he had to resort to heavy labour for an income.

We lived in that place for up to eight months, growing more and more distressed at how our move for a 'new beginning' was, on the whole, unwinding as an expensive endeavour. Just before Christmas in 1984, Clive's former boss in Sydney telephoned us one day to see how we were going.

"Clive, how is the family? Have you got a job yet?" he asked.

"No," my husband replied. "Thing's haven't gone quite the way we would have liked, yet."

They talked for a little while when his boss said; "We're missing you, mate. We've still got your job here. You can have it back if you're interested."

The news heartened Clive considerably, particularly as the promise of stable work could mean the opportunity to get on top of escalating finances. He said he'd consider the offer and afterwards, we discussed our present situation against the practicality of returning to Sydney. In the end we agreed that in the following January he would return to his old job while I would stay on with the kids and attempt to sell the house. For the next ten months we listed the house with several real estate agents but were unsuccessful in finding a buyer. The distance and indefinite duration of our time apart worked on us until it was almost unbearable. I could not report any progress on the sale to Clive because, as we eventually discovered via a good friend, the agents were actively discouraging clients from buying it.

Clive was frustrated at not being able to be with me in dealing with the agents and when I told him of their under-handed behaviour, he was furious. He left his job and came back to us in the October of 1985 and we removed the property from the agents' books. We tried two more agents in the next few months to come, but it was the same old story, "Sorry, but no-one has enough money these days". Though reliable work was still quite difficult to find, all members of our family were now receiving an income of sorts enough to sustain the bills.

By around mid April of 1987 we met an English real estate agent who was new to the area and who was looking for some business to get him started. We told him of our earlier dilemma with the local agents and he asked us to let him try, promising us that, if we let him "handle it his way", he would have it sold by the end of the month. Reluctantly we agreed and in three weeks he had scheduled an 'open house', in which an offer was made right in the first hour of inspection. Thirty minutes later we had a second offer that was slightly better than the first; we took it and within six weeks we were packed and ready to move, by the first week of June we were off our family was again on our way back to NSW. We stayed a few days with friends before leaving W.A. but we have no doubt 'someone' was watching over us that day.

୫୦୧୫

Warning from the Mother-in-Law

In early August of the same year after returning to the east coast we bought a small house on the Central Coast of NSW and were able to move into it by late September 1987. In the months of trying to sell the West Australian home, the younger of my two son's, Kevin, had fallen in love with the daughter of some friends there. We weren't aware of how close they had become, so that by the time we had settled into our Central Coast home and with the arrival of Christmas several weeks later, he announced she was coming over to visit us. Her stay would last for up to three months in which they intended on getting engaged on the first of January, 1988.

This was a shock for us, because we didn't expect him to go into this sort of commitment so soon and had even thought they would have forgotten each other over time. She arrived in late December and they celebrated their engagement as planned. She left in March and three months later in the June, to our sorrow, he moved back to W.A. to be with her. Although happy for him, we were all too aware of the distance between us, which would mean few opportunities to visit with him, he stayed with her family until well after they were married.

They married the following March in 1989 and have lived in W.A. to this day, they moved into their own home after their first child was born, then again to a different location after their fourth child. We only see him on special occasions, either over there or over here and we do miss him terribly. He now has five children and the opportunity to share in their upbringing is something we've sadly missed out on. I love those kids and I have found it a dreadful experience not seeing them growing up, or of playing with them, or even going for walks with them on any given day.

In 1995 Kevin and his wife made their first visit back to us, but it was on their return to the city airport for the home trip that my mother in law warned me of an impending death. We were commuting from Sydney Central to the domestic flight terminal via the airport bus and as we passed the area where Peter – my husband's brother – lived, she said quite distinctly, "*Peter will be coming over soon.*"

'How soon?' I asked, rather automatically.

I had not even been thinking of her, or him, though there was no doubt of her voice speaking to me just as if she had been seated there in the bus, too!

"*In about three weeks,*" she said.

I felt weird while we waited at the airport and I couldn't help myself in telling Clive and Kevin what I'd heard on the way. I think they were in disbelief, but they accepted my thoughts then Kevin and his young family boarded the plane and went on home.

Exactly three weeks later we were told Peter had been admitted into hospital. His wife was a nursing sister and was able to describe his condition to us. It didn't sound good, so we went to visit him, knowing my mother-in-law's warning was near. When we arrived at the hospital ward he was heavily sedated and in and out of deep sleeps and he wore an oxygen mask. While we were with him, I became aware of someone with me. I couldn't see anyone, but I just new I wasn't alone.

In fact, I could sense quite a few people around me and my first thought was that his Mum, Dad and oldest brother, Leo were there. Or was it someone entirely different? It didn't really bother me, all I knew was they had come to help him over. He was in and out of slumber a few times while we were there and in one of these sleeps his wife and my husband went out of the room.

I stayed behind to try and help him to pull through, mentally speaking to him, telling him not to give up but to fight and to get better for his children's sake. Peter opened his eyes and smiled, then closed them again and clutching my hand, he gave it a gentle squeeze. An hour on and we left the hospital for home.

Whatever I'd said must have worked, because a week later he picked up. Two weeks later and he was allowed to leave the hospital. But one month on he was admitted into a hospice, where he survived for a further four weeks. Incredibly he maintained a positive attitude despite it all.

"I hope you get better soon," I had said to him once.

"No," he replied. "I won't be walking out of this place – they'll be carrying me out."

"Oh don't be like that," I gently chided.

"No," said Peter reassuringly. "That's what the morphine's for."

On reflection, I think he was willing himself to die. Morphine is typically given to terminally ill patients to help them cope with their physical pain and sadly his condition declined. Three months exactly from the time I had heard my mother-in-law's warning, he passed away there. I feel he had been meant to go earlier, but I had talked him out of it, if only to give him a 'second chance' for his kids.

Now at peace, Spirit had allowed him those two precious extra months to say goodbye to his family and friends. I suspect Peter greatly appreciated this 'gift' too, as I myself did, for not enough of us get such an opportunity for last words to be shared.

Almost another three months went by and, while getting ready for bed, Peter 'dropped in' for a visit.

"*So that's what you look like?*" his voice came through the room all of a sudden.

Silently I froze, conscious of wearing only my underwear.

'*Go away,*' I told him, '*or maybe turn around, because you are being rude!*' and mighty quickly I whipped on those pyjamas.

"*Thank you for everything,*" he said, with genuine gratitude.

"*That's okay, just don't watch me getting dressed again.*"

"*I'm sorry for being rude,*" came the parting comment. I'd say his mother caught him out, too, for I gained the impression she had told him off. I've never heard from him since.

ଚୟଓଷ

For the nearly ten years we lived there, we only felt and sensed the presence of others, or had glimpses of different apparitions. On one occasion my daughter, Christine, was preparing to travel to far north Queensland and wanted to take her beloved pet budgerigar with her. I felt uneasy about the journey, for I 'knew' the experience would be unpleasant. In due course, the budgie suffered a haemorrhage and died at one of their campsites, devastating Christine.

Four weeks passed before her return to us, but in that time we picked up her thoughts that she consciously sent to us. There were specific hours of the day to which we could match her whereabouts and moods, a mental connection reaching both my husband when at work in Sydney and myself at home on the Central Coast. When she was able to find a public telephone, (this was before mobile phones were readily available), she'd ask us what we had been doing or thinking at a particular hour or day and if we had 'thought' of her. We could confirm the same timing and she would tell us what she'd 'sent'.

৪০৫৪

While living in our home on the Central Coast we often heard strange noises, or saw glimpses of someone walking around. One day Clive and I were having lunch at the dining table. A side window positioned at a right angle directly next to the back door allowed us easy view of anyone standing on the back step. Unexpectedly a fair-haired man with fair skin, who looked around thirty-ish, approached this rear entrance, surprising us because visitors could only come to the front door; access to the back was blocked by a padlocked side gate.

"Looks like we've got a visitor," Clive whispered suspiciously.

"Yeah," I said, as he got up to meet the person.

On opening the door, no one was there – they had simply vanished.

"Oh-oh, there's no one here!" he said, alarmed.

We agreed to check both doors as well as the front and back yards, with Clive muttering about prowlers. We found no signs of anyone, concluding it had to be a 'ghostly' someone. Soon it occurred to me that my late nephew, who was also fair-haired, had passed away in a fatal car accident some twelve months earlier. He was close to thirty-two years when it happened. Was he the one calling to say hello?

৪০৫৪

The Mystical Dream

In putting together this book, I was only going to talk about my psychic experiences with people in spirit, but after many months of writing and rewriting and realising the vast wealth of experiences I've had that include more than just communicating with spirits, I came to understand that the following dream, too, came from the other side. It was mid August in 1997.

I walked out the front door of this very stately mansion, down a wide pebble-stoned driveway, where I noticed two small children ahead of me; a boy around the age of five and a girl of about seven. I think I may have been a Nanny to them, for it seemed they were not mine. Huge iron gates fronted this house and we walked out of them, turned right and started up an old country style road, just a little wider than a one-lane road.

As we approached a left bend a short distance away, I realised the children had gone and as I glanced around, looking for them, I noticed in the paddock to my left a lot of mist. I wondered if the children had gone over to investigate it, because I could hear child laughter coming from the area. So I approached the misty paddock and went into it, moving down a gentle slope until coming out the other side, where the ground slightly inclined.

Here, gothic type buildings stood like tall apartments in dingy, dirty streets, reminding me of a scene from a Sherlock Holmes movie. It was dark as I walked down one of these streets and I realised there was no one around and it was eerily quiet. Ahead was a corner leading into a very large square, where talking could be heard. It was daylight there and as I entered the public square I noticed people looking at me, as though simply observing me without actually speaking to me.

It was almost like being in London looking at Buckingham Palace, for there was an enormous building similar to that of a palace straight ahead. A huge, black iron fence surrounded it and as I gazed up at this place, I saw people everywhere – on the ground, on the rooftop, some even appeared to be floating up and down between the roof and the ground as though they were in an invisible lift, without wings or any ropes to lift them.

I gained the sense that I must have lived in this dream-world and had never seen this building before in the daylight – apparently the township only 'came alive' at night. I found the odd behaviour of the people levitating between floors very intriguing, so much so that I had long forgotten about the two children and sat down on the pavement into a lotus position. With my hands at either side and palms flat on the ground, I tried to push myself up, but this didn't work so in despair I lowered my head and tried to fathom it all.

I suppose I began to meditate, for, as I concentrated on their floating abilities, I felt myself move. This freaked me a little but it also felt strangely good. So I tried a bit harder and moved again. I found that as I relaxed it was easier to lift so I closed my eyes and thought of flying like the people at the palace. Before long I became aware of not feeling the ground beneath me. Curious, I gently opened my eyes and saw I was now very close to the merlons atop the palace roof.

I was thrilled! I knew now how they did it! It was only a thought wave for them and they were there! Here I was three stories up and with the world at my feet, looking through merlons in the wall to the flat roof beyond and then, from the new heightened view, taking a good look around at the grounds below. I glimpsed the two children running across the front lawn of the palace, heading towards the iron fence.

Duty called me to return earthward and on landing I ran after them. As I'd guessed, they were heading for home, the mansion beyond the mist, so I tracked close behind them, through the large iron gates and the public square, down amidst the dark and dingy streets – when I sensed we were being followed. Several people were hurrying towards me, as though trying to stop me from going back home. Though no words were actually spoken, I was sure they didn't want me to tell other people 'out there' of this dreadful place.

The children disappeared through the heavy mist in the field so with a burst of speed I hastened to catch up to them. But the people of the gothic town were closing in on me. I kept wondering; would I get home safely? Will the children be alright? Or will these scary people catch up to me and drag me back? Maybe they will kill me? Who knows?

Finally I made it into the mist and out the other side, where the sky was a shade brighter than when I first entered it. It seemed we had been gone for most of the night and now I worried what the children's parents would think of me keeping their youngsters out. Looking round to the mysterious paddock, everything had vanished – the mist, the people, even the village. Now I was alone in the middle of nowhere, not knowing where to go or what to do. Did this really happen? Was it a dream or had I travelled to somewhere on the other side?

Just then the alarm sounded. I had to get up to see my husband and son off to work. I couldn't shake the realism of the dream and repeated it in detail to Arthur. He insisted I write it down and one day write a book on it. He felt I had visited the dark side very briefly, as a warning for the future. These days – at thirty-five years of age – he was more open to psychic and supernatural occurrences.

"Hah!" I scoffed, "it's not long enough for a book!"

Although I hesitated a great deal on it's length or even value for this book, I had been busy with some notes for *My Encounters with the Spirit World* when very clearly I heard my son's spirit say, '*And don't forget your dream of the mist! You've got to put that in there too!*'

Certainly there may be comparisons between images and symbols in it with what we may believe the other side contains and every part of this dream – to this day – feels exceptionally real and vivid. Why did it affect me so? Why stay so strongly in my mind years later? Perhaps, as Arthur had suggested, there were messages in it from Spirit and perhaps a warning for looking after one's own safety. Someday I know it will make full sense to me.

ᘒᘓ

Chapter Seven

MY BELOVED SON

Farewell, My Son

The year of 1997 was a bad year for a lot of people, even for the queen herself. We had fires, earthquakes, even a landslide at the Snowy Mountains ski resort, where Stuart Diver was the only survivor. Around this time my oldest son, Arthur, had prepared a little garden in the knee-high brick wall right by the front door.

"I hope you don't mind, Mum," he'd said that afternoon. "But I planted some flowers in there." One of Arthur's greatest pleasures was tending the garden; growing vegetables, even propagating a thriving carnivorous plant collection.

"No I don't mind," I had replied, (as if I was ever going to get around to doing anything with it anyway!). "Go right ahead."

On the 31ˢᵗ August, my birthday, the world received the awful news that Princess Diana had just been killed in a shocking car accident. Arthur adored her like a lot of people did he watched her funeral on the following Saturday this was his birthday. In Australia, Father's Day fell on the Sunday immediately afterwards.

Keep in mind Arthur had been trying to quietly cope with mental health issues for a number of years now, however this should bear small affect on his feelings in the wake of Diana's death – it seemed everyone was unhappy. Mother Teresa had passed away only the week earlier and in the April, Tasmania had experienced horrific trauma with the mass shooting at Port Arthur. All of these events, collectively, had left a harsh impact on him.

Add to this he was now thirty-five years of age, single and living at home with us. Although not a father himself, he had always longed for a wife, a soul mate he could cherish but who seemed elusive in this life. I understand now he had been suffering severe depression, anxiety, as well as schizophrenia.

We all shared a small chocolate cake his sister, Debbie, had made for him for his birthday, though he didn't eat much food at all. We said goodnight around eleven o'clock that night and went to bed.

"Try not to worry too much, she's in a better place where no one can harm her now," I remember saying to him of the Princess. "Go and have a good night's sleep and we'll see you in the morning." I then gave him a kiss on his cheek and a big hug and hoped he would be okay the next day. But it wasn't to be. I wasn't to know this was the last time I was to hug my son.

About an hour later, around midnight, I noticed his bedroom light was still on. My husband was in a deep sleep; however I was uneasy, worrying about Arthur. I felt someone was telling me to go and check on him, though regrettably, I thought I may have just been over-reacting and dismissed it. I was reluctant to go into his room in case I might have intruded on his privacy, so I continued on trying to go to sleep, not knowing what he really was up to.

I must have started to doze off around one-fifteen, because I didn't hear him sneak out of the house. But a dreadful noise abruptly woke me shortly after. I first heard it coming over the railway crossing, located about five hundred metres away. The warning horn of a north-bound inter-urban train blew a continuous howling, growing louder as it came closer. Horrible experiences have a way of running in slow motion, in which every miniscule detail will be noticed and lay a permanent imprint in the memory.

The urgent warning took on a 'gurgling' aspect, like water being poured down a funnel into the train's horn. I wondered what on earth was wrong with the train driver for at this time of night, he would wake the neighbourhood. I could hear the train's wheels screeching as though they had locked up and were now sliding on the tracks; it was clear the driver was desperately trying to pull up. The sound of metal grinding on metal seemed to go on forever – I thought it would never stop. These eerie, awful, scary sounds curdled my stomach, even as I recall them today, the memory leaves me feeling fearful and sick.

And then it happened, directly across the road from our house – literally opposite our home.

THUMP!

A chill raced down my spine.

My husband sat straight up and screamed, "My God, he's hit something or someone!"

In a blinding rush he raced outside and crossed the empty, two-lane road to the knoll where a standard wire fence partitioned the public off from the train line, but where sizeable gaps left room for established trees. I changed into a dress, (absurdly, I didn't want to risk being seen outside in my pyjamas), for, in the back of my mind I was concerned he could go into shock with what he saw and that he may need medical help. I was right.

As I headed for the front gate my husband stumbled back in, white as a sheet and crying, "It's Arthur! It's Arthur! The train hit Arthur!"

"Don't be silly, it couldn't be," I said, looking toward his bedroom. "He is in his room, see? His light is still on!"

"It's Arthur I tell! I know it's Arthur!"

After settling my husband down on the lounge, I walked to Arthur's room to be sure.

"It *was* him," Clive insisted. "When I got to the fence, another goods train was coming very slowly down the other line to Sydney. I saw who it was from it's headlight."

Those images scar my husband to this day. I couldn't believe my ears; this was our first-born son, now dead, broken into pieces on a cold and filthy track. I had to see it for myself to believe it was true. But first my husband needed me, so I helped him to the lounge and made him rest. Stubbornly wanting to prove Arthur was in his room, I then walked to his door, quietly praying – hoping – all the while I would see him in his bed. He wasn't there.

Yet, as I was opening it, I felt a strong backward pull, as though someone was trying to warn me of the biggest disappointment I could've had that night. The bed was empty, except for some envelopes neatly placed on top of the blankets (these turned out to be messages of love for us, telling us why he died). It seemed Arthur's spirit was trying to hold me back to avoid the pain of reality.

Trembling, I went very cold, determined now to check the train line to confirm it *was* Arthur's body over there. On my way to the front door I found Clive clutching at his chest. He had rung for an ambulance but, on seeing me, begged me not to go over.

"No, I have to see it for my self," I insisted. "I have to *know* that it's *not our son* the train has hit!"

I ran next door to where my daughter, Debbie lived and banged on her front door to wake her.

"What's up?" she asked. It was about one-forty in the morning, so she was very sleepy and hadn't apparently, heard a thing.

"Arthur's just been hit by a train. Get over there [pointing to our house] and look after Dad. He needs someone to watch over him – he's having a heart attack!"

I left, too wound up with fear and confusion and just hoped she would do what I asked. But I could not let it pass that my beloved son might really be on the tracks – surely it was something else the train had hit, wasn't it? Even so, the goods train had reversed back to the station some three hundred metres in the other direction. I assumed the drivers of both trains were waiting for the police to finish surveying the area as it was very dark. Then I noticed a torchlight in the distance, coming from behind the rear-end of the inter-urban train.

"Hello!" I called out to the person in a very loud voice. "Was it an animal or a person the train hit?"

"What?" came the reply from the other side of the tracks. I decided to be more direct.

"Did the train hit a young man with a beard?"

"Why do you want to know?" they called.

"Because my son's missing from his bed and I am worried it may be him!" I anxiously replied.

"Go to the front of the train and see the constable in charge, and tell him what you have just told me," he replied.

I thanked him and immediately hurried up the road toward the station, hoping it wasn't my son but instinctively knowing better. I became aware of grass being walked on and turning around, saw Debbie right behind me, following me instead of going to her father's aid! I was furious!

While waiting to speak with the constable, I noticed a lot of railway men standing around, presumably discussing the situation. They saw me and called for the constable in charge to help me with my questions.

"Could you tell me if the train hit somebody?" I asked as soon as I could.

"Why, what's it to you?" he checked, not impolitely.

My words tumbled out in a rush; shock was setting in. "Well, my husband and I heard the train hit someone or something, and my husband raced over to the fence and reckons he saw my son on the line, but I'm not convinced and my son is not in his bedroom!"

"What does your son look like?" he asked very calmly.

"He's thirty-five years old, with short, black curly hair and has a reddish beard." Right behind this I added, "My husband's having a heart attack and he needs an ambulance!"

"Where do you live?" he asked in the same calm voice.

"Down there where the light is!" I pointed to the house – so evidently close to the crime scene.

"I would like you to go on home to be with your husband. I'll send this ambulance for your husband as we don't need it now, and then come to see you when I know more."

On returning to my home I found Clive clutching his chest, trying hard to breath. Moments later the ambulance arrived, with the men tending him quickly. Some ten minutes passed as they worked to stabilise him and they were just preparing him for leaving for the hospital when the constable's fatal knock came at the door. I froze, afraid to hear the worst.

Please say it isn't Arthur, I thought as I moved to answer the call. *Please say it wasn't him Clive saw. Please don't let it be him*. I was still hoping I was going to prove my husband wrong and that the constable was going to say something like, "You don't need to worry yourself, it wasn't your son but another young man that resembled your son's description. Maybe your son just went for a walk." *That* would have been really good news, the kind of news a parent would rather receive, but no, not this time.

"Hello," he said steadily. "Can you tell me – did your son have a white, terry-towelling dressing gown?"

I swear my heart dropped like a lead weight. I knew I was in for bad news because Arthur wore just such a dressing gown. "Yes . . ." I replied. "Don't tell me it was him?"

"I'm afraid it was, Mrs. Duncan."

I think I went blank.

"Do you want to come in and see my husband?" I asked.

He accepted and I led him into the lounge room. Then, amazingly, a very calm, warm feeling came over me and it felt as though someone was giving me a big hug. I assumed it was my beautiful son reassuring me that he was now at peace and no longer in any pain. I also sensed family in spirit around Clive, trying to comfort him. Even though I couldn't see them, I know they were there – I could *feel* them.

When the constable realised he could do no more for us, he asked to see Arthur's room, where he asked me some further questions about him, then prepared to leave, saying it would be a good idea if I went with Clive to the hospital.

I was reluctant for a few reasons, not the least for which our two young Maltese dogs would be left in the house alone.

"No, I couldn't go and leave my little puppies locked in the house," I said, (incidentally, Honey, the female pup, had spent the whole time Clive was fighting his attack on his lap, intently focused on 'healing' him with many licks). "I'd prefer to stay home with them," I added.

The paramedics insisted I go with Clive in case he needed me. I didn't understand why they wouldn't let me stay home until the next morning; the constable came to the hospital to see how we were coping and admitted to us then that they were worried I would have gone over to the railway fence (or line itself) after the ambulancemen left for the hospital Though it had really bothered me to 'see the facts for myself', they weren't to know I would not have gone to the line out of respect to my son.

By two o'clock I telephoned Kevin, my other son in Perth, Western Australia to give him the sad news. He was devastated and said he would fly over here on the earliest flight.

It was a long night. My husband survived the attack and the next morning he was allowed to return home. Debbie arranged for a friend to collect us and when we arrived at the front door of our home, I noticed a bright flush of red in the brick-walled garden. One lone flower had come into full, glorious bloom, striking me with its beauty and gentle simplicity and it reminded me instantly of Arthur. In fact, it seemed to capture the essence of who he was and I had to question the uncanny timing of its appearance, for none of the seedlings he'd planted were flowering yet. Certainly none were in bloom the day before.

In the days leading up to his funeral, the flowers came out one by one.

80C3

My beautiful son, Arthur, taken in 1990

The Days that Followed

That same Monday I made many phone calls, a tiring duty to give family and friends difficult news. One elderly lady refused to believe me. She was a member of the church that Arthur had attended and whom she considered him as very special.

"He can't be gone," she said in a matter-of-fact tone. "He was just here having a cup of tea with me. I saw him for his usual morning tea, so he couldn't be dead!"

"But he is," I replied, as gently as I could. "He was hit by a train just last night."

She went on to explain how she had been making a cup of tea at around ten a.m. and when she turned around to go to the table, Arthur was sitting in his usual chair. She wondered how he had come in so quietly, or that he hadn't knocked at the door, yet she didn't question him because she trusted him.

That was the way with my son, everyone who knew him knew he was honest and trustworthy. She asked him if he wanted a cup of tea; he smiled and nodded. She then poured it out and chatted to him awhile.

"But the strange thing was," she added curiously, "he just smiled at me, not drinking his tea."

She wondered why this was so and thought he might have needed more milk. So she went to the fridge and on returning to the table, discovered Arthur had gone.

"I was hurt," she said, with confusion in her voice, "because he didn't say goodbye and I thought I must of upset him."

ಏﬡ೧ೞ

It wasn't until the funeral that losing Arthur had finally sunk in. Even Kevin's arrival (minus his young family), had not brought the devastating reality home. It was not just that he had died, it was *how* he had left us which made the grieving so hard. We were reluctant to tell people he'd gone under a train by his own choosing, perhaps because the image this presents can be quite shocking to the listener. Too, we are of a generation which shies from the ugly word of suicide. Certainly it is not a clean death and the people who have to recover the remains must have to dull their emotions and somehow learn to block out what they find. You would have to detach your senses or else your mind would go insane and I feel for the people who helped to retrieve my boy that night.

Thank you, all of you and on behalf of my son, who we know was not wholly thinking properly at the time, he too, is grateful (this conveyed from spirit). Our hearts also go to the driver who could not help stop the train that night. We *know* you tried, we know you had never meant to hit him. We sincerely hope you have come through this experience alright; please understand you are not responsible for what happened.

I know Arthur was trying to communicate to us in the days and weeks, even years, following his passing, but for me, due to the promise I had made on his behalf so long ago, my reception to him was blocked off. This hurt me far, far deeper than I could ever have dreamed. Even so, there were many signs to say he was with us, like the day of the funeral . . .

As we gathered in our driveway where the lovely flowers bloomed, some relatives noticed a yellow airship (used for business advertising) flying directly over our house. There was also a vintage bi-plane which happened to fly very close to our house, performing some aerobatics. Arthur's passions included airships, historic and fighter planes, flying in these vehicles, as well as the colour blue and yellow. We took these sightings to be his way of saying he was still with us.

As a family we chose to give the mourners the opportunity of seeing him in the coffin before the service. I understand some people find this idea abhorrent, but we all agreed how there would be those who loved Arthur who would not find closure without this final viewing. He meant a lot to a great many people and subsequently the chapel was crowded to 'standing-room only'.

It is interesting to note that frequently, with those who die from a train hit, (particularly in pedestrian impacts as compared to say, collisions with a car), the victim's head is horrifically scarred, damaged, or quite possibly unidentifiable. We were blessed with Arthur's face being wholly presentable, barely scarred and if he were bruised, then the morticians who prepared him did an expert job on covering any blemishes. We cannot help but wonder how much of Spirit's hand had something to do with this . . .

A good friend and florist arranged the floral wreath I had requested for his coffin; a huge cross lined in his favourite colours of yellow and white gerberas (for peace and purity), 'blue' orchids for his love of this colour (which were actually violet shades, but the association was to the sky, violet, however, indicates a strong spiritual/psychic connection, too) and red roses down the centre (because he loved red roses and for its symbolism to blood and deep, deep love). Sprinkled through the roses were 'Baby's Breath' sprigs, for he was not only my baby, it was also a symbol of my beloved son's breath. Green ferns were blended throughout the arrangement and brought the whole thing to life.

After saying our last goodbyes to him, my youngest daughter, Christine, made a very good request – one I will treasure until my dying days. She asked if it would be okay to take a photo of him and the beautiful flowers before they put the lid on his coffin. I was alright with it as long as the funeral directors had no problems with it, which of course, they didn't. After she took some pictures, they put the lid on and away we went to the chapel for his service and all along we were wishing for some kind of sign to say Arthur was happy at what we did for him, not realising just how close he was to all of us at that time. We didn't know until one week later just how significant those pictures would be.

⁎⁎⁎

During the gathering after the funeral in the outside courtyard our nephew, Leo, came to share with us his condolences and floored us when he revealed how he had seen Arthur on the day he had died. Leo lives among heavily forested mountains near Bellingen, N.S.W. a six-hour drive from our home (before the main highway was upgraded).

"I was confused at what had happened to him," he said. "I thought something must have been wrong."

"Why was that?" my husband asked.

"Well, around one-thirty p.m. I was standing on the veranda looking over the valley and I saw Arthur coming up and he had these huge wings on. I thought he was going to a costume party. As he was coming up to the house I thought it was strange he was walking up and not driving up to the house where the driveway is."

Leo's house is perched on a steep slope, where the back veranda looks onto a narrow valley formed by a creek. There's a three-metre drop between the veranda and ground and to get down there he has to either go out to the front door and around the side of the house, or via an internal staircase – both of which blocks his view of the rear yard.

"I wasn't thinking clearly," he added, "and went down to the back door to greet him . . . and when I opened the door he was gone!"

He felt perplexed because the vision was so clear and yet nothing could be seen of Arthur afterwards. It wasn't until the next day he was given the news of his cousin's death by a relative.

ℬℭ

One week later, just before Kevin was due to return to his family in W.A. Christine showed us the photos she took of Arthur and the coffin at the viewing. My heart raced and I knew my prayers were answered when I saw the ghostly image of a white bird flying up and out from the centre of the floral cross where it lay on the coffin lid. (*see picture on page 120*)

No one at the time actually saw the bird yet it stands out unmistakably in the photograph (taken on a standard imaging camera of the day – digital photography wasn't available to us then). Christine readily gave me the picture to keep, (she still has the negative, where the dove can be seen there, too!) which I took to a local clairvoyant.

I was surprised to hear this lady say she recognised him, (she was taken aback herself). She had read for him only the week before his passing! She wouldn't reveal the details of his reading due to client confidentiality, but explained the bird was his way of showing his spirit leaving his body, that he was now free – he had got the wings he'd said he would have one day. She wasn't to know the relevance of her words.

As an infant Arthur regularly drew wings. From the age of five, pictures were carefully sketched by the week and in his eighth year he brought home from school a true masterpiece. A huge pair of golden angel's wings on a black A4 sheet. It took my breath away, I could instantly tell he'd put his heart and soul into every meticulous feather. The detail was incredible and finite.

"I did this at school today," he'd said.

"Aren't they beautiful?" I replied, unable to take my eyes off them.

"Yes, I'm going to wear these when I grow up and die."

"What?" came my shocked reply. He had seemed quite convinced, so matter-of-fact about it.

"Yeah," he repeated. "I'm going to wear them when I die."

It was as though he had a higher being talking to him, perhaps telling him this was so. Back then I wasn't into spiritual or supernatural happenings and I was stunned, horrified to hear such talk coming out of a child's mouth, let alone my own son's. I had forgotten this conversation in the years that followed and to hear the clairvoyant speak of Arthur having his wings at last brought it rocketing back to me. When I added Leo's sighting of him through the forest as well, happiness surged through me.

"This was his way of saying goodbye," she finished.

∞

Two nights after the funeral, Debbie had been visiting with us and now ready to go home, asked if someone would mind walking back with her. Kevin and I accompanied her and at the end of her driveway we stopped to talk some more, reminiscing about our son and brother and of how we missed him terribly.

The conversation, naturally, was all about him being in spirit, for we all firmly believed Arthur was there with us as an invisible presence. The sky was cloudless and starry and the air became very still. It smelt as if a fire was burning somewhere, though neither smoke nor flames could be seen. It was a strange atmosphere that had come upon us.

"I wonder what Arthur would say now if he was looking down on us?" Kevin said, continuing the discussion. "I wonder if he's sorry for how he left us, I wonder what he –"

All of a sudden we heard a loud, thunder-like bang and across the road some thirty metres away we saw a flash of light just like lightning hit the telegraph pole. All of the streetlights went out, but no houses lost power.

Debbie screamed and clung to us, though Kevin burst into laughter at her fright. We thought it uncanny the timing of the words with the unexplained phenomena. Sure it was an alarming moment, but Kevin couldn't stop laughing.

"This has gotta be his way of telling us he's around," I said, trying to contain my own giggling (well, it *was* funny). I looked up to the night sky and said gratefully, "Thanks Arthur."

The burning smell and calm air immediately vanished and the street lights all came back on. Despite trying to calm Debbie, she eventually went inside quite shaken. Kevin and I were still laughing about it as we entered our house.

"What happened?" Christine and my husband, Clive asked, their faces curious.

We relayed the experience in detail.

"I wondered why Debbie screamed out the way she did," said Clive.

"I heard the bang," Christine noted, "and the house lights flickered very briefly."

"I heard nothing," Clive added. "But I did notice the street lights were out. I thought we must have had a blackout!"

It was a touching emotion among us that night to know we had nothing to worry ourselves over wether or not Arthur was alright. He was still with us and at peace.

৪০০৪

My son's coffin with the spiritual dove rising above (circled) –
please note: except for the circle, which is placed exclusively for illustrative purposes, this image has NOT been manipulated

Luke and Melissa's Friendly Ghosts.

On a fine afternoon some months later I had a surprising phone call from Kathryn, a niece living in the Sydney area, about a one-hour's drive south of my home. She was worried with the odd behaviour of her young son, Luke and knowing of my background in spiritual matters, thought I might be able to detect if he was seeing a ghost in his room.

"I'm worried about Luke," she began, a little hesitantly. "He is frightened when he goes into his room because he can see something, or someone and runs back out. I don't know what to do for him. Can you help me please Aunty Joyce? I'm worried that whatever or whoever it is might be wanting to harm him."

Pausing to call upon my guides and angels for help, a picture emerged in my mind of what looked to be a friendly sort of man. He was smiling, so I knew he meant no harm to the family.

"Don't worry," I said to her. "He is perfectly safe. He has a tall, thin man watching over him and I'm sure he wants Luke to see him. So tell Luke when he sees the man to just say "hello", and he will take care of the rest." Then I had a vision of Kathryn's younger child, her daughter, Melissa, who at only a few months old, I sensed wasn't very well.

"By the way, is Melissa lying on the lounge?" I asked.

"Yes Aunty Joyce, why?"

"Oh, no special reason, and has she got her head at the kitchen end of the lounge?"

She paused, then answered, "Yes. Why?"

"And is she facing the hallway?" I persisted.

"Yes," she replied, with frustration in her voice. "How can you tell? You are not here to see her."

I went on to explain to Kathryn how sometimes I get visions when on the phone to people – sometimes they are strong and sometimes they're not. In this case, they were very strong. I felt this spirit-man was related to her partner, the father of Luke and Melissa and that he wanted them to know he was with them.

"Has Phillip's father passed over in the last three or four years?" I asked.

"He's been gone four or five years now . . ." she commented, clearly thinking it through. "He died just before Luke was born. Why?"

Going on what I could see of this little baby on the lounge, I added, "Is Melissa smiling at the hallway and stretching out her hand as though to touch someone?"

"Yes! You are spot-on!" came her excited reply. "She is! Why?"

"Because I can see the man trying to reach out to touch her. Because she isn't well, he's trying to heal her. He's trying to hold her hand to make her feel better, for this is his way to heal her. That's why I asked if she was holding out her tiny hand. She is happy to see him."

I heard Kathryn's sigh of relief and sensed calmness come over her.

"I feel this must have been arranged with them in the afterlife before she was born," I said, very pleased I'd made the connection for her. "Don't worry about the children, for I feel Phil's father will stay with them and keep them safe for a long time, because he loves the kids and will look after them."

"That's great! Thanks Aunty Joyce. While I'm at it, the other day when I was in the lounge room, I looked towards Melissa's bedroom and I thought I saw the silhouette of a lady wearing a corset from inside her room, walking past the door. I went down to check it and there was no one there! Can you tell me who that was?"

I tuned into the bedroom as best I could, searching for the mysterious presence. I saw the mist-like silhouette of the lady in question, standing in the corner, in period dress. She appeared to be smiling at me as she was becoming more visible, so I tried asking her who she was. She had the quiet, gentle, reserved attitude of women of her era, so even though she wasn't 'talkative' so to speak, I received the impression that she was related to Phillip, such as his grandmother, or Great Aunt. As with the spirit-man, she showed no animosity towards them but rather, was keeping an eye on the youngsters.

"Gee, thanks Aunty Joyce! That's great," Kathryn replied after I told her the details. "So I won't worry myself about seeing any people? And I don't have to worry about the kids anymore?"

"Yep, that's right," I said. "The kids are being watched over and will be kept safe."

"Thanks Aunty Joyce. I'm glad I rang you, I had confidence in you to help me out. I knew I could rely on you!"

It was a job well done, which made me feel great. Mentally I thanked my guides and angels for helping me and our call came to a close a little while later. Fourteen years on and the kids have grown into bright, healthy teenagers, with Luke holding a steady job and Melissa doing well in high school. Kathryn's father passed on early in 2011 and he, too, is watching over them.

෴

An Uncle's Visit to His Favourite Niece

Approximately five months later in early 1998 my younger son, Kevin, rang me with incredible news; his oldest daughter, Linda, had something she wanted to tell me, (she was only seven at the time and didn't know Arthur very well, only that she was his favourite niece).

"Hi Nanna! Guess what happened at school today?" she said to me excitedly on the telephone.

"You got an award," I replied jokingly.

"No, but Uncle Arthur came to see me," she uttered.

A chill ran through me.

"Really? What did he have to say to you?" I went on.

"Well," she said, "I was trying to work on a difficult question in my schoolbook, when I looked up and saw him. I asked him if he could help me to solve it because it was too hard for me. He came and stood beside me."

I asked her, "Did you speak out loud enough for the class to hear you, or only in your mind?"

"I hadn't thought about it at the time," she said, "but I think it was in my mind, 'cos no one looked at me."

"And did he help you very much?"

"Yes!" came the reply. "He stayed with me until all of the questions were answered and I got them all right! The teacher was very pleased with me, but I didn't tell her that I had help from Uncle Arthur." Then she said something that took me very much by surprise. "And, he had his girlfriend with him."

Few people who'd known Arthur closely were aware of what he'd wished for before passing over; to find and marry a soft-faced, blonde woman with blue eyes. In his final twelve months he began telling us he had a girlfriend of this description waiting for him in spirit and her name

124

was Sara. Only Clive, myself and Christine, (and possibly Debbie), had been told these specific details. He'd even went as far as to scratch a love heart on the tree outside of our Central Coast home with their names "*Arthur Loves Sara*," on it before passing. Yet here Linda had described her perfectly.

"Did he give you his girlfriend's name?" I asked.

"Yes! Her name is Sara!"

There were many times after this in which she told me of the numerous occasions where she needed help and she merely had to think of him and he would be there to help her, especially with mathematical sums. Now at eighteen, married and with a young son of her own, she has said how her baby often talks away as though he is having a conversation with someone else, whom she feels is her Uncle Arthur. Her husband has reported seeing him in both his dreams as well as in spirit form and though he has never met Arthur, I feel he must have been shown a photograph of him at some stage to have recognised him.

80C3

Within the next two months or so I received another surprise phone call from my younger sister, Brenda, who claimed to have had a strange dream the night before, involving Arthur . . .

"I was floating into your house," she explained, "then looking down on you in the kitchen where you were cooking sausages and eggs for breakfast. Arthur came in through his bedroom door, wearing Clive's tartan dressing gown."

Clive did have a tartan dressing gown during the years we lived in the Hills district of outer Sydney, though with much use it wore out long ago.

"You asked him if he would like any sausages for breakfast but he shook his head, saying that he didn't like them. Then he turned around and went back into his room." She was curious and wanted to know if this had happened when Arthur was alive.

"Well, yes, a long time ago, sort of, but I don't know if he ever wore Clive's dressing gown. Besides, we don't eat this sort of meal now, not for years!"

Brenda insisted he was alright and of how real the experience was. I didn't want to deny her, you can't tell what another person did or didn't see. But I did doubt my abilities to tune in to Spirit, particularly where my beloved son was concerned. Perhaps, for Brenda, it was knowing she'd seen him and, importantly, that he was going to be fine.

༺༒༻

Keeping a Promise

On a night six months following Arthur's death, Christine, had an experience that would change her life significantly. She was living on the Mid North Coast of N.S.W. and though she had been asleep to begin with, a ghostly figure came to honour a promise made to her before he'd passed. I have asked her to tell you her story of this night in her own words . . .

Hello, my name is Christine and yes, I have seen a real ghost. There's a distorted perception of the word 'ghost', so let's get this sorted out right now. What we see in movies or T.V. is, unfortunately, a typical exaggeration of truth for the sake of getting you glued to the screen and sometimes, the depiction of dead people are incorrectly portrayed due to the complexities of story-telling on film. Either way, 'ghosts' are not bad – you could even say they don't exist – because everyone in death becomes a spirit *again*. Be it enough to say this is a subject for discussion in another book and here I will keep to the task at hand, for it has relevance to Mum's psychic experiences.

In the fallout of a person's suicide the days, weeks and months can be a violent roller coaster of emotions. Time might not stand still for everyone else, but it sure stretches thinly for the people left behind who try to come to terms with their loss. The questions flow unendingly; was it me? Did I cause him or her to die? Where are you now? Are you alright? If only I'd listened, or paid you more attention, or whatever it was that you needed from me. You can go crazy in an attempt to make sense of it all and I, too, was no different.

I wanted to die myself. I wanted so badly to see where Arthur had gone, to know what it was like there and to be assured he was no longer enduring the daily horrors of demonic torture and religious sanctification. In the end I had to realise the act itself is the other person's decision and no one – *no one* – is either responsible for the death nor likely to have been capable of stopping it. And in Arthur's circumstances, no one could have in this, his final attempt. Again, suicide is a subject to be covered elsewhere and I urge those of you who can identify with our story to seek company in counselling groups of similar experience.

Because of Mum's psychic abilities we kids naturally developed a bit of interest in it too and more than once my brother and I agreed that, whoever died first, he or she would come back and show themselves to the other to prove there was life after death. I don't know if he'd planned to be the first to go in our younger years and certainly I hadn't seriously considered dying until I'd reach old age. Even so, in grieving his loss and fearing for his well being, I spat the spiritual dummy – big time.

I was furious I couldn't 'see dead people'. I couldn't hear them, I wasn't being given any near-death experiences I so desperately wanted and it seemed nobody in spirit cared. Everything I'd heard about relating to spirit guides, angels and deceased loved ones etc. apparently made an exception in my case and this was grossly unfair. It might sound daft to say, but in the days immediately following his death, I had actually been receiving thought-communication with Arthur a number of times. My 'inner eye' could see him smiling, or frowning and at the viewing on the funeral day I distinctly sensed him crouched before my father as he cried to the body in the coffin. It was also my camera and I which captured the vision of the dove flying up from his body *(see picture on page 120)*

It was a dreadfully sad occasion and among the very worst experiences I've ever known. Back then I didn't understand how psychic abilities worked; I had a programmed set of beliefs that weren't playing out according to my expectations. It came to be, one late afternoon toward the end of January 1998, that I parked my car in the garage after finishing work for the day and told the Almighty *exactly* what I thought.

It was mean, demanding and punctuated with several unpleasant words not fit to include here. Be it said that God was copping a serve. And not just God. Everyone I had thought existed in spirit and were willing helpers in this life of mine got a mouthful of rage too! Dear Arthur wasn't excluded, either.

Through pouring tears and a heart breaking with unbearable pain I gave them an ultimatum – Arthur, show me yourself in spirit form or I turn my back on you all! I meant absolutely every single word. They knew – God knew – that I would close myself to any belief in an after-life and in the existence of GOD himself. I swore an oath for all who witnessed this tirade that I wouldn't sway in opinion for the rest of my days if proof of spiritual life wasn't granted to me. And to ensure they were given plenty of preparation I included, "You have within these next twelve months to do it."

Part of me can laugh a little nowadays at the memory; I was demanding the All-creator to 'cough up or else'! However, much more of me understands the depth of pain, doubt and fear I was feeling back then and with my developed abilities today, they let me 'see' what they saw and it is with tremendous compassion these beautiful loved ones stood by, listening, grieving with me and loving me despite the outburst.

When I was finally satisfied that my conditions were verbally, loudly announced, I went in the house and downed a few glasses of whiskey – oh yeah, an excellent way to close a meeting with God . . . Yet I deliberately chose to put the matter aside after this because to think on it consciously at every other moment was both foolish and futile – if they had any salts worth, they knew I was waiting. So the weeks went by and summer turned to autumn and in the wee hours of the night on March 16th of the same year, my eyes flew open at the sound of a burglar.

The entire house was raised about a foot from the ground, timber-floored and carpeted, with timber posts, fibro-sheet walls and corrugated iron on the roof. Many of the windows were of the old-style wooden frame, which could be easily opened due to a lack of the more modern dead-lock bolts. Covered beneath numerous blankets and pillows, I listened as footsteps creaked from the lounge room to the hall right outside my bedroom door.

So convinced was I of an intruder that my hand began to slide over the mattress for the long stick nearby, which I was wholly prepared to belt around their head once they were close enough. Meanwhile, my eyes stared through the gap in blankets and pillows at the door, a discreet spying for the anticipated brute that would be seen due to bright moonlight as well as streetlight illuminating through the blinds of the bedroom window.

A figure did appear, just within the entrance, but not clad in black beanie, skivvy and jeans. The outline of a male became visible against the backdrop of walls and door, clear as glass and facing me in silence. As I stared, it moved forward to the end of the bed and then 'slid' to its left so that it was standing in line with my feet and body (it was a double bed with me currently on the right-hand side, my feet closest to the room's door and my head furthest away). By this point the figure was undeniably really there, for detail now enhanced its features.

I was looking at Arthur.

The best way I can describe for you to grasp what I saw is to refer to Kevin Bacon's character in the movie *Invisible Man*, where on two occasions he is 1) wet from the pool, a 2) surrounded by steam. Both give you an idea of looking at 'glass', so to speak and I know there are other movies that use similar techniques or have much the same special effects, however this is the one that first comes to my mind when I think of this magical moment. And this movie wasn't screened until well after March 2008.

Arthur was beautiful, young and serenely quiet. He stood there for as long as he could manifest his presence, I'm certain and though I couldn't measure the minutes exactly, it *was* a considerable length of time he was there. Initially my mind wanted to analyse this apparition, wanted to doubt if what I saw was for real. I recalled Mum saying in numerous conversations about psychic abilities that one of the most important things to put aside is your logic, because Spirit doesn't work to the same laws that govern our physical plane.

Because I cared for my brother's attempts, (which were quite possibly something he was still learning how to do) and because I had so strongly desired a visual encounter with him, I consciously ignored the doubting inclinations and simply 'went with the flow'. I believe it was because of this approach for which our time together was so meaningful, since I was then provided sufficient opportunity to 'study' his appearance.

Arthur had left this world aged thirty-five, with a man's fully-bearded face that seemed to constantly show fear and profound sadness in every line, wrinkle and curve of expression. The face before me this night was youthful; a blended mix of his brother Kevin's similar looks but which otherwise harkened of black hair and brown eyes and suggested to me an age of fourteen, perhaps fifteen at most. He wore a light blue shirt that had twin rows of buttons down the chest-front and brown corduroy pants – both of which he wore in our childhood. I remember thinking while I watched him . . . *yeah, I recognise those clothes! You wore them in the seventies!*

Arthur's gaze seemed focused on the light coming through the closed blinds of the window. I sensed he was seeing his own spiritual plane rather than my earth one, almost as if others were watching him from a few yards away – elders or his personal guardians who had given him 'permission' to show himself to me. I am forever grateful they did – I thank them now and always for having heard my plea, for understanding my heart's needs and answering it. I love you all.

After a while his image slowly, gently faded, leaving me high with love, respect, fascination and wonder. Never had I known the brilliance of seeing – truly *seeing* – a spirit, a someone who had actually walked this earth and was now physically dead. Glimpses of hands, or spirit lights, the sensing of others as they passed by fleetingly had occurred too few and far between for me. But not this. I thank you, beloved brother, for keeping your promise.

I love you, soul mate.

Always.

And thank you, dear reader, for sharing this experience with me. Love, light and blessings to you all.

Lastly, thank you Mum for allowing me – encouraging me, to include this insert in your book. I love you, too, Blessed One.

႘ဢ.

Chapter Eight

FAMILY LOVE

Catching a Bus to Heaven

My mother was aged around eighty-one when she began showing signs of Alzheimer's disease and by age eighty-two was placed into a nursing home – only 3 years before Arthur left us. She went in under the impression she was going to rest 'and get better', after which she believed she would come home again. Of course this wasn't to be; we knew she wasn't happy living there, probably because she didn't like hospital environments, where one was confined to a bed, as she eventually was. Unfortunately none of the family members were sufficiently equipped to care for her medical needs and professional help was the only answer.

In January 2000 – almost three years after Arthur died – when her mind had significantly deteriorated – she experienced a severe fall from her bed and was rushed to the local hospital for treatment. Mum often had little falls but this one was particularly bad and instead of recovering, her condition worsened. She didn't recognise anyone and couldn't speak, in fact she hardly opened her eyes. She was also in and out of deep sleeps. Phlegm caused her to choke constantly and the hospital staff had to keep clearing it with a tube.

Over the following week her health declined rapidly and late on the Friday afternoon my husband and I drove the hour's distance from home to see her. My sister, Hilda was there already and by the time visiting hours were closing, I approached a nurse to ask what Mum's chances were of seeing the night out.

"Very slim," came the reply. "But don't worry, we'll ring you if anything happens."

That's when I made my mind up to stay with her – I didn't want to be woken up at two or three in the morning to be told she had gone, or had died whilst we drove back to the hospital. Clive understood my dilemma and agreed to me staying behind while he returned home to the Central Coast.

"Could I stay with her?" I asked.

"Go and see the Sister over there," she said.

"Would it be possible for me to stay with Mum, because I have to travel a long way in such a short space of time, only to be told I am too late?" I asked the Sister. "Could I sit in that armchair next to her bed?"

"Yes," she said. "As long as you are quiet and don't disturb the other patients."

"If you're staying, I'd like to stay too," Hilda said.

The sister seemed to consider the situation; the space around the bed was limited and a medical team would need all of it. Also, I think they were worried we might disturb the other three patients in the room.

"Okay," she agreed at last. "So long as you're not both in the room at the same time in case we have to get to her in an emergency."

My sister, Hilda and I chose to take turns with Mum and I was to have the first watch while she tried to rest in the waiting room down the hall. The nurse gave me a thin blanket and pillow and at first I felt strange settling in the chair beside her. Very quickly I realised why – not only had I never slept in a hospital chair before, but the number three was now beginning to haunt me.

Mum was in bed number three and her ward, also, was number three. This numeral has frequently occurred in my life and I knew it meant something, but what? God had appeared to me in the wardrobe mirror three weeks before receiving the doll for Christmas and at that time we lived in Thirteenth street. We attended three out of four family deaths within a five month period. We lived in W.A. for three years. My brother-in-law Peter went into hospital within three weeks of his mother warning me and died three months later.

Every fifteen to twenty minutes the staff would come by and check on Mum, clear her throat and turn her over. It seemed to be a ritual and I was feeling quite sorry for her situation, as well as helpless because I couldn't do more for her but just be close in case she needed the staff in a hurry. Some two hours went by. As I sat closer to her and held her hand, I found myself praying to God to take her away from all of this misery she was going through. I reflected on all of the good times and the bad ones I had experienced with her while growing up.

I realised that it must've been very tough for her leaving her family behind in the homeland all those years ago, bringing her husband and four kids to a strange country and not knowing anyone. Her own mother died five years after we arrived in Australia. She wasn't able to go back to

England for the funeral – and now I was faced with losing her. At least distance and money weren't going to be a problem for me when laying her to rest.

Eventually I settled back, yet continued praying for God's help. I realised I was really begging for her mercy, asking Him to forgive her for all the wrongs she may have done in her life and to make her transition into Spirit easier, where those she'd loved and lost in death would be waiting for her.

Suddenly I noticed a greenish mist, or vapour, appearing over her, in between the space above her neck region and thighs. It rose up to a foot (30 cm) off her body, when I observed a very tall man materialising on the other side of the bed near her head. Visible only from below the neck, I sensed he was her father, who had died when I was seven years old. On his right side a small, petite figure appeared – her face included and joy filled my heart.

I knew this woman. She was my beautiful Grandma. (Mum's mother). As a child I looked forward to visiting her, for she would always join in with my attempts to tell silly jokes around the fireplace. She was a patient woman and great to us kids. My last words to her on the night before we left England were, "By Grandma, see you again soon."

Of course I didn't have a clue just how far we were going, only that it would be 'a long journey'. To my sorrow I never saw her again and I missed her terribly. Happiness filled me now to see her – if only in spirit form at my dying mother's bedside. She smiled my way and I smiled back, then she looked down to Mum and began stroking her shoulder.

A third glow emerged at the foot of the bed and, to my delighted surprise I saw my Dad – her husband of thirty-four years – standing there. But this was to be an exceptional night for me, something so totally unexpected that I forgot all else in the room, the hospital, or even time itself. My beloved son, Arthur, came into view left of Dad, trying to look reverential yet, it seemed, hard-pressed not to smile at me. Both stood there quietly with hands clasped in front, as though patiently waiting for Mum to pass over. They even had a gap between Arthur and Grandma just wide enough for Mum's spirit to fill.

A large number 'three' took form in this space, amazing me. The green mist (or ectoplasm, as it is more commonly called) continued to rise and I knew Mum's soul was leaving us. I'd heard of such phenomena occurring before and apparently medical staff see it often in operating theatres when a patient dies. But until tonight I'd never actually seen it with my own eyes, surrounded by family very dear to both of us.

Reality seems to have a habit of rudely jolting you when you least want it. Hilda burst into the darkened room just then, unable to sleep in the waiting room due to feeling cold and because too much noise filled the corridor. She also thought I might have needed a break. How mistaken could she have been?

The view around my mother's bed was blank – everyone in spirit had disappeared and I wondered . . . did it really happen or was it my imagination? Physically Mum wasn't dead yet and I wasn't game to tell Hilda what I'd seen in case she thought I was going mad. Perhaps Spirit must've asked Mum if she was ready to pass over and maybe she hesitated enough to stay behind with us, no doubt wanting the family together to say their goodbyes to her. Who knows?

Even so, I let Hilda take the seat while I went for a short walk.

When I returned to Mum's room the nursing staff had brought in a second chair for me, where I was able to sit opposite Hilda and, to my amazement, was in exactly the same spot where I saw my beautiful grandmother.

From here I was able to see the night sky through the window. In my mind I imagined God was there amongst the stars and I sent Him a big "Thank you" for allowing me the experience of some twenty minutes earlier. I felt I was blessed to see something so very special.

The next morning my sister went to get a cup of tea in the small room down the corridor where she overheard two doctors talking about Mum's condition. I walked in as she was asking them about the type of medication Mum was on.

"We're giving her morphine for any pain she might be having," they said.

"What would happen if you stopped giving it to her?" we asked.

"She would not survive very long as the disease would kill her."

"Wouldn't it be kinder to let her go with dignity than let her linger on this way? Giving her medication to keep her alive is cruel and costing the government money. Why can't they let her go naturally? She's suffered enough."

"We're not allowed to watch her die, but to help her live as long as possible – that's our job."

"If she was an animal," Hilda went on, "they would put her to sleep. So what's the difference?"

"Even if we did what you wished and the rest of the family found out, we could be in a lot of trouble," they said.

"Don't you worry about the families," we both piped up. "We'll handle them. They'll understand!"

"Okay," they replied, with tremendous reluctance. "We'll stop the medication if you insist – with your permission. You'd better get the families together because it'll only be a matter of time."

"How long do you think she will last without it?"

"Possibly eight to ten hours, as she's riddled with the disease."

"Please, go ahead and stop all medications," we asked, formalising the agreement. Knowing Mum would soon be free of her suffering gave us a great sense of relief. She could pass on with dignity rather than lie there as a shrunken old woman – limp, frail and oblivious to the world. We began contacting the various family members.

The first one to arrive was Hilda's oldest daughter, who said, "I can only stay for a little while as I have to go back home to the Central Coast. I have things to prepare but I will be back later."

I asked her if I could catch a lift with her as I needed to shower and change and it would save my husband the ordeal of finding things for me to wear. She agreed, for it was also company for her on the long trip home. On returning home I also grabbed lunch, which made me feel much better, then went back to the hospital, this time with both Clive and Debbie, who still lived next door to us.

In two's and three's we gathered around Mum's bedside to say our farewells and simply wait for the inevitable. By early evening Mum started choking and the staff rushed to clear her throat. This happened a few times during the course of the evening visitors hour and as there were young children visiting their own relative in the room's other bed, the sound, particularly for them, was frightening.

Hilda's friend – a male nurse (who worked in a major Sydney hospital) – insisted on Mum being moved to another room away from the other patients. Seeing the children's reactions, they shifted her to the holding room next door. At least here the space was quite considerable and many of us could surround her unencumbered. Eight o'clock brought visiting hours to a close and graciously we were all allowed to stay by her side, though presently Clive and Hilda's oldest son left to check on their cars.

Debbie sat beside Mum, holding her right hand when I felt the strongest urge to go and talk to Mum about crossing over.

"Do you mind if I hold Mum's hand?" I quietly asked, "I need to talk to her."

"No, go ahead," she replied, letting go and sitting back in the chair.

Leaning forward I whispered close into my mother's ear, wanting no-one to hear what I knew was both intimate, as well as highly sensitive in nature.

"Hello Mum, it's me again. Can you here me?"

Of course there was no visible response since she was sleeping, but I knew this was perhaps the perfect chance I had to help her pass on in relative ease. I wanted to convey to her the image of riding in a vehicle which would take her to the other side where she now belonged. I knew she hated travelling by train for she had been a passenger on one that had derailed near Doonside, N.S.W. in the early 1980's.

Inspired by the movie *Heart and Soul*, in which the characters who'd died had to board a bus to go to heaven, I said, "Can you see that bus over there on the other side of the road?" Using visualisation techniques, I saw us both standing on a busy street corner, where a bus waited across the road, filled with her relatives who had already died and who were smiling at us through the windows.

"If you hurry you can catch it," I went on gently, "because they are waiting to take you over to their place. They are going to have a big party for you, with dancing and lot's of cups of tea to drink!" Mum loved her tea and dancing and most of all, parties.

"Can you see who's on the bus?" I asked. "There's your Mum, your Dad, your sisters, my Dad and look – there's my son in there too! Can you see them? They're all waving at you to hurry up 'cos they can't wait much longer and if you miss this bus you'll have a very long time to wait for the next one. Go on Mum, go with them now and we'll see you later. Go and have a great time with them all and give them all my love. Bye Mum."

I gave Mum's hand a little squeeze and let Debbie take hold of it again. Walking away, I noticed Hilda and her youngest daughter looking at me with a bewildered expression. Did they hear what I'd said? Hilda sat down beside Mum as I continued to leave the room, ignoring their curiosity and keen to find my husband, whom I badly needed right then.

I heard Mum choke badly just then and looking around, saw she had fallen limp. It seemed to me this was her way of telling us she was hurrying across the road, sure to make it to the bus in time. I went to get Clive and my nephew to tell them she'd died when Hilda cried out, "Oh no, she's gone! Quick! Someone get a nurse!"

From the hallway I gazed at Mum lying so peacefully on the bed, certain she'd caught the bus and happy she was now on her way to the after-life.

'Goodbye Mum,' I mentally said. 'Have a safe trip and thank you for listening to me.'

Someone rushed past me for the nurse and a little way down the hall a voice called to me from the holding room.

"Don't worry about getting the men," a young woman called, "They've got her back!"

I was furious. I could see Mum being pulled backward just as she was about to get on the bus and she was frustrated with the physical hold for her to stay on here in a worn and useless body. I gave them a feeble wave but ignored the request. I wouldn't listen and resolutely left to find Clive, hoping Mum's personal will to rejoin her lost loved ones would prevail and their desire to receive her in spirit would see her succeed no matter what.

I met Clive in the car park and told him of the news, so we hurried back to the ward. We were told Mum had returned for only a couple of minutes and then 'went again' – this time unable to be revived.

Now I was satisfied; she'd finally got on that bus and was riding to heaven with her loved ones. I wanted to shout, "Good on you Mum! You finally made it! Thank you for fighting this. You are now free of suffering." Naturally this would not have been received as happily by her teary children, grandchildren and the fellow-aged, ill patients of the rooms around us.

"She finally won the big one in Lotto," I remarked instead, since it was being drawn right about then; it seemed appropriate. "First prize, a trip to heaven."

This didn't go down well either, but inside I understood a very different scene to what the others were probably thinking. Then the spooky number '3' fell into place; Mum died on the 31st January 2000, Dad died thirty years earlier on the 13th of January 1969. She was in ward three, bed number 3 and she died at 8:35 p.m. Add this to the other occasions where this number has appeared and perhaps you can see why it's significant to me.

∞∞

My Mother, Hilda Duncan, taken around 1961

A Guardian Angel

In coming to terms with Arthur's death we attended suicide bereavement groups and talked with others who had lost loved ones this way. Although it seemed to help initially, we were advised not to make any sudden or rash changes – like moving – for up to the first twelve months at least. This is to avoid regretting any 'let downs'; decisions made under emotionally-charged circumstances that may or may not evolve in a negative or disastrous way. This is not a hard-and-fast rule, since a loved one's death can sometimes be the catalyst to achieving goals we might otherwise have been putting off. It's a rare thing to advance positively in the wake of losing those dear to us and most people find themselves less than better off when making such impulsive decisions.

For us, staying in a house which *I* no longer wanted to be in, with the very spot where he died on the train line right across the road from our front bedroom, where both freight and inter-urban trains went past every twenty minutes or so, choosing not to move was a serious and genuine health risk. I insisted to Clive on selling up and leaving the entire area – there were far too many memories of our boy here and too, the local population had grown far beyond its original elderly community. It was now a bustling, emerging young city with expanding families and too many youths driving their cars noisily along the streets.

Then of course there was the scheduled rail timetable of the inter-urban City to Newcastle train – the last ride north for the night – which continued to drive past at around one-thirty in the morning each and every Monday. Without fail we'd be awake when it went by, reliving the horror in the dark. Often Clive would appear to be asleep, but I'd hear the soft crying or sniffling nose in the dull quiet that followed.

At least one train of this busy line would be making some sort of squealing noise in the course of *that* night and I cringed inside with the knowledge it was slowly killing us. Almost weekly we'd hear reports of people who had died accidentally or deliberately by train-hits around the area – up to six people in our locality within five months alone, not including Arthur. One of these was only six hundred metres down the road at the level crossing, early in the evening of December 1997.

In June 2000, three years on, I was in a deep sleep when I became aware of an approaching freight train coming down the line. I heard a very loud screeching noise in the distance, the sound exactly as it had been on that fateful night in September '97. As it drew closer, I sincerely hoped Clive wasn't hearing it too, but my hopes were shattered as the freighter passed the house noisily.

Just when it seemed unbearable, he sat up straight and screamed, "Oh no, not again!"

Mercifully no one was killed and we don't know why the train was breaking so heavily and while it seemed to take an eternity for this hulking chunk of metal to get on its way, it took me two hours to convince him and settle his nerves. Unfortunately it happened again the following week – not quite as noisily – but enough to stir those ghastly memories. He suffered a heart attack and ended up in hospital for a week and a half. Back home again and two days on another heart attack returned him to hospital, this time for a two-week stay.

"Can you work out what is causing these attacks?" the doctor asked.

"I think I'm reliving my son's nightmares," he replied.

"What is wrong with your son?"

Clive gave him the background. Clearly the doctor was moved.

"I will let you go home on one condition," he said very firmly, "that you go and pack your bags and move away from the area."

He came home the next day and I immediately put the house on the market. We notified Christine in Taree and began making several trips to her, utilising these visits to look for another house we could move to. Once or twice I travelled this distance on the XPT and on one of these trips my seat, (again, number three, which was not intentional), was in the Sleeping Car.

The seats were built in cubicle form and due to a reasonably empty carriage, I was able to sit at the window. Feeling strangely alone, I kept the door of my berth closed and enjoyed a quiet ride for up to an hour. Then a lady I had never met before came in, taking her seat across from me and starting up a conversation as soon as she'd settled.

"How far are you travelling?" she asked.

"To Taree," I answered. "To visit my youngest daughter."

"I'm going to the border of Kyogle."

"That's one place I am thinking of looking at to live," I happily said.

"No, you don't want to live there," she gently warned. "You will be better to stay nearer to your youngest daughter. Why do you want to leave the Central Coast?"

I explained the predicament of our situation, including how I was praying to God that we would sell it quickly and she understood.

"No, you don't ask God to help you sell it," she instructed, "you thank him for selling it."

"But we haven't sold it yet," I replied, confused.

"That's not the point. You must say "thank you for selling my home" and he will look after you."

At the time I thought it was a silly idea but took what she said on board. Yet the weirdest thing happened on leaving that train. From outside on the platform at Taree I turned to wave goodbye to her, only now there was no one in the seat where she'd been, nor in the cubicle at all. I couldn't say whether she'd gone to another part of the train or if I had just imagined meeting her; there was no sign of her anywhere.

&OCS

In looking to buy our new home, we always felt someone in Spirit was with us. I was most conscious of Arthur's presence, of course, as he knew what we were looking for – what we needed and what would best suit us, too. We saw pictures of two houses in the Taree district and asked the agent to see them. Although I really liked the first house, Clive was uncomfortable about its steep driveway. The second house caught us instantly. We fell in love with it and laid down a deposit as soon as our offer was accepted.

In waiting for settlement to take place, however, our Central Coast house was yet to secure a satisfactory tender (negotiations were in consideration). Concern and frustration bothered us because we needed the sale of one to buy the other and we feared losing the Taree property before the closing deadline.

Remembering what the lady on the train had said, I made sure of *thanking* God for *selling* the Woy Woy house. Meanwhile, I think Arthur put in a 'helping hand'. The final day of settlement arrived and it seemed we were going to have to withdraw, loosing both our deposit and the Taree home, when the agents call came in.

"We have a couple interested in your house – they've agreed to buy it for the price you asked," she said.

"Do you mean . . ." I began, hardly believing my ears.

"It's sold!"

In the end it was a quick sale, as I'd wanted. Three months after we put it on the market it was sold also the mysterious XPT encounter, in December we moved to our new home. I couldn't stop thanking all the spirit people for helping us to sell up and move. I've heard how Spirit can work in mysterious ways, bringing people and objects at the most fitting times or through uncanny experiences. Sometimes these people are called Guardian Angels, because they bring you messages from Spirit. I've never seen this woman again and I feel she had to have been my guardian angel, giving me the direction I needed to make the right decisions. I also feel this might have been my late son's gift to us, for there were many 'signs' relating to this property that suggested his presence was strong here.

⅚⅛

Kevin's Vision At Work

Late one afternoon in 2003, I received a telephone call from my younger son, Kevin, who was at work and sounded quite down. But he soon said something that lifted both our hearts.

"Hi Mum," he began. "I was feeling pretty miserable at work this morning."

His work duties included sweeping up broken glass off the floor. He worked in the factory of a company, who made specialised sheets of glass. It was a menial, yet hazardous job and with the heat coming from the metal roof throughout the day, it could also be quite stifling.

"I hate this place – I want out," he grumbled.

"Why, what's up? You sound depressed," I said, wanting to coax him into talking.

"I am. I just wish I didn't have to come here. I've had a gutful of it." He gave a frustrated grumble. "Hey, you wouldn't guess who I saw today – Arthur!"

"Yeah?" I asked, rather excited to hear more.

"Yeah. I came out from a row of crates that hold these big sheets of glass," he explained, "and as I passed this open doorway nearby, I had this funny feeling that I had to look *up*. Now, these crates can stand three metres high, but at the top of the one right next to the door was Arthur! He was only visible from the waist up, but he was smiling away and it was like he was trying to say "It's alright, Kev, I'm here". I couldn't believe it!"

"Do you think he was trying to put your mind at ease?" I stated questioningly, pleased to hear him happier at talking about his brother.

"Yeah, I think so. I've been wanting out of this job for so long now. It gets really hard putting up with the nonsense and the bullying in this place, but I don't know where I can go! It's not like I can afford to leave here. I've been trying to work out how to deal with it, but I'm getting nowhere!"

"Did he say anything?"

"No. I looked around quickly to see if anyone else was nearby – which they weren't, thank goodness – and when I turned back, he was gone! It was incredible! There's no way he could've been up there if he was alive, Mum! You just can't get up that high without a crane or a ladder!"

"So why be so miserable? I thought you'd be on top of the world!"

"Well, I am, sort of," he answered in frustration. "I want to see him again. I've been wanting to see him since he died and now he shows up at work – after all this time!"

"But that's wonderful, Kev. At least you've got to see him!" I said, trying to encourage him. "I've only seen him once when Nan was in hospital, but I don't mind. In fact, I was honoured to see him again since he's gone, if only because I'm his Mum!"

"I know," he softened, "I was just hoping that if I could see him once I'd be able to see him again. I mean, why can't I see him all the time? Why is it so difficult?"

"Well, sometimes it's not that easy for spirits to show themselves to us," I reasoned. "Often it's a case of "the right time in the right place", as the saying goes. Give him a chance down the track and he'll probably appear to you again."

"Yeah but why can't that be now?" he insisted, clearly disappointed.

"Maybe you need to be ready. Maybe it's a case of not *thinking* about it so hard and just letting it happen when it happens."

"Yeah, well, not seeing him again has left me even sadder," he muttered unhappily.

"If it's of any help, Kev," I said, wanting to reassure him and lift his mood, "I feel that Arthur has been trying to comfort you from the other side on many occasions. He's with us all as we need him. Just accept the fact that you've been blessed to see him already."

₴৩ কৈ

Arthur's Birthday Gift

Apparently though, he was around us on all sorts of occasions. Debbie took me to a card reader in Ettalong on the central coast of N.S.W. (just before the move). It was a lovely gift shop with crystals and jewellery and other interesting objects commonly found in New Age stores. While waiting to sit with the clairvoyant, we browsed the shelves, finding many things we'd love to have bought yet trying to contain ourselves at the same time. I felt a strong pulling towards the corner opposite where I was looking and a familiar voice came to me.

'*Go over there, Mum,*' Arthur said.

Slowly I made my way around to the area where I was supposed to be, curious about what he was so excited to show me. Christine, his youngest sister, loves fantasy – anything from dragons to fairies and especially winged horses and unicorns. She also likes strong colours such as black trims on furniture or red fabric, for example. I felt compelled to look up and then I saw it.

Right there on the wall before me hung a beautiful clock; it was round, with a unicorn painted on it and trimmed in black.

"Oh, isn't that beautiful?" I whispered, breath-taken by the picture.

'*Please get it for Christine from me,*' Arthur begged. '*It'll be my gift to her.*'

Christine's birthday was around a month off, but I noticed the price and my heart sank.

'*I'm sorry Sweetie, I can't afford it mate,*' I mentally replied.

'*Ask Debbie to help us buy it,*' he urged. '*I know she will.*'

So I called her over to me and told her how Arthur had asked me to buy the clock for Christine. "But I can't afford it," I said.

Debbie seemed surprised and without hesitation she said, "If Arthur wants it, then I will buy it for you and you can pay me back later."

He was right, she did help me and without me telling her that he said she would. Christine loved her present and smiled knowingly when I said who it was really from. After hanging it up with a fully-charged battery, she noticed it's unusual ticking sound.

"Mum," she said one day, "you know that clock Arthur got you to buy for me?"

"Yes," I answered. "The one with the unicorn?"

"Yeah. Well, it's got a funny way of ticking. Not every second will be heard. It'll tick for some seconds, go quiet, then tick a few more. It doesn't seem to work the same at exactly the same part of the clock with every cycle. In other words, you'll only hear it tick hear and there at random."

I thought it was a bit strange though smiled. Nothing would surprise me with Arthur these days.

"You do realise the odd thing about all this, don't you?" she went on, grinning suspiciously.

"What's that?"

"When he was alive, one of the things we used to talk about was space and time – science fiction stuff, where things like wormholes could be a portal through time to other galaxies. But we also talked about how the realm of Spirit exists *outside* of our time – the way we humans measure time, like past, present and future. Where God is, where we go when we've left this life – it's all free of *time* as we know it here. Time doesn't exist there!"

"Yes?" I asked, wondering what she was getting at.

"Well, what an interesting way to confirm it – show me a clock that doesn't *sound* every second yet keeps real time? You could think of it like this: time is measured here and these are the seconds in the clock we hear ticking and time is *not* measured *there* and those are the seconds we don't hear ticking. Get it?"

I'm not sure if I did entirely 'get it', but like I say, experiences involving Arthur in spirit don't surprise me and if this is how Christine interprets a gift given from him *after* he'd died, then I who's to argue? She's never found any problems with it aside from the unusual ticking and that's *with* using more than one full-charged battery.

ဆာ၈သ

J. B. Duncan

The Unicorn Clock bought for Christine on behalf of Arthur

Chapter Nine

SECOND CHANCE

The Adopted Mother

In January 2008, Hilda and her twin brother, David, along with his close friend, Heather, came to visit us. When after our dinner the conversation took an unexpected turn.

"Would you read for Heather, I told her you can read cards," he said.

"No I can't. I haven't read them for years," I said, waving it off as a bad joke. "I've lost it."

Apparently he found that humorous.

"Bulls__t!" he chuckled. "Of course you can! How can you lose it after all these years?"

David didn't know of Arthur's plea to me so long ago, nor did I think I could have explained it to him, but I am sure he wouldn't have understood.

"He's told me so much about you," Heather said with excitement. "I can't wait for you to read mine. But if you don't want to I can understand, seeing as you don't know me."

It was true, I'd never seen her before this night and I honestly didn't think she'd get much of a reading with me.

"I gave my gifts away years ago," I said. "I could give it a go if you really want me too, but don't expect much from me."

"That's alright!" she insisted, still as enthusiastic. "Why not? I'd love to see how you go!"

It's funny to think that, despite so much time away from the cards, I kept them in the top drawer next to my bed. They were precious to me, still in their original case and it was with reluctance I took them out. I sent a little prayer up to my guides, asking for their help, hopeful I would pick up something from Spirit.

I had no idea of what was going to happen and asked her to shuffle the deck, think of the things or subject most important to her and place them face down on the table. Then I proceeded to turn them over and hopefully they would reveal something of importance for her, I sat there,

152

staring at the cards while struggling to make sense of the arrangement. I'd almost forgot how to read them! Nevertheless, perhaps some things never truly leave us.

While pondering on the meanings and interpretations before me, I noticed a pair of lady's shoes appearing on the floor next to my right foot. I saw her ankles become visible, her legs and as I scanned upwards, the hemline of her skirt. I realised I was now starting to feel the presence of the lady and her entire image could now be sensed in my mind. She had fair hair and a softly-spoken voice, which revealed insights into Heather's background.

'*I am her mother,*' she said.

"Has your mother passed over?" I asked Heather.

"I don't know," she replied. "I was adopted when I was pretty young and only saw my real Mum on occasions."

Dutifully I reported the spirit-woman's visual presentation.

"It does sound a lot like my adopted Mum's description. She was beautiful and she died a few years ago."

'*She often gets depressed and needs comforting,*' the mother said.

"Do you have a room in your house with lavender walls and a chair next to your bed?" I asked.

She looked at me with a worried face and gasped, "Yes, I do! Does it tell you all that in the cards?"

"No," I replied. "She is standing next to me and is telling me to say this and she said that you get depressed a lot. Is this true?"

"Yes, that's right! I do get down quite a bit sometimes! I miss her so much," she cried.

"Well, she's telling me to tell you that when you are feeling down you are to go into your room and sit quietly in the chair and think of her, because she is trying to speak to you, but you don't hear her."

Heather took a deep breath and said, "You are good, because this is what I do whenever I feel lonely and down. I'll try and think harder of her next time."

"Don't think too hard," I suggested. "Just relax and let it happen. Listen for voices in your mind even if you think you are just imagining it. Just acknowledge it and accept what you hear and it may make sense to you."

She seemed to understand everything I said to her and was very pleased with the rest of her reading. When I was finished she hurried outside to where my husband, daughters, brother and sister were gathered and told them how good the reading was.

"She was spot-on with everything!" she declared.

Quietly I packed my cards into their box, mentally sending a big "Thank you" to all of my guides and angels for helping me. I was so happy to learn they hadn't left me 'in limbo'.

෨෪

Kevin's Dream

Nearly five years later – nearing the tenth anniversary of Arthur's passing, Kevin had a very unusual dream, which he hoped I might be able to explain what it meant . . .

He was standing at a bus stop, though he didn't know why. An interstate coach pulled up and when the door opened, who should step down off the stairs but his beloved brother. Kevin burst into tears, leant forward and gave Arthur a mighty hug.

"How are you, mate?" he asked him. "Where have you been?"

They began walking down the street, with Kevin still chatting.

"I'm so pleased to see you again – I didn't get to say goodbye to you before you left us!"

Arthur had never replied and after a moment Kevin realised Arthur wasn't beside him, so he turned to look back, thinking Arthur was lagging behind because he may have been tired.

But Arthur was gone.

That's when the alarm clock went off, ending the dream as Kevin woke up, feeling quite frustrated.

"Why did he disappear, Mum?" he asked over the telephone. "Why didn't he say anything?"

"I think Arthur knew how you were feeling, for you must have been thinking of him lately," I said, attempting to tune in to Arthur's spirit.

"I think of him constantly! Almost on a daily basis, especially when I'm working in my workshop!" he replied.

"Then," I went on, "I feel Arthur came to you in your dream to reassure you he had not forgotten the good times that you both had shared and that he is never far away from you and this was his way of allowing you to say your goodbyes to each other."

Kevin seemed to accept this answer. To this day, though he's still wanting to see him again with his physical eyes, he says he often feels Arthur around him and has also had many dreams with Arthur in them.

Maybe one day . . .

⁕⁖

Slowly My Gifts Return

By 2007 Christine and I regularly attended the local markets, selling our crafts and fantasy giftware to the people who love their dragons, fairies, angels and such. At one of these events we met this beautiful lady who was also selling similar items. She and Christine connected instantly – both shared interests in the fantasy genre, in the metaphysical world and psychic abilities. Perhaps it helped that only a month separates them in age, too. Christine was learning how to read dragon cards and the lady – also called Christine – was already skilled in reading standard tarot cards and Reiki work.

"I used to read ordinary playing cards," I said, "But I don't do it anymore."

"Oh, why?" she asked.

I told her my story of how I'd lost my gift. "And I don't know what to do to get it back," I finished.

"Ah, we can fix that," she assured, smiling. "Close your eyes and repeat this prayer after me."

She softly recited the words and I repeated them, while the two of us held hands and bowed our heads respectfully.

"You should meditate as often as possible," she added at the end.

"But it's impossible for me to sit and meditate for very long because my husband is around too often!" I said. "He'd be wanting his cups of teas, or be busy in the house or yard and be making a lot of noise and this will disturb me. Or the phone will ring or the dogs will want to go out!"

"Why don't we meet at my place for weekly meditations?" she suggested.

It was a wonderful idea and as soon as we could arrange the best times, Christine and I went to the other Christine's house and began our sessions. The first few weeks were wonderful; an intimate setting of four people in a room lined wholly in candles. Soon we were joined by Meg, a medium who would teach us in psychic abilities, for our group expanded to seven. Just prior to her first visit with us, Meg telephoned my daughter for the time and locality details, yet while they talked, I was standing at the kitchen sink washing up when all of a sudden two spiritual elderly ladies appeared at my left side. They wanted me to give Meg – whom I'd never even knew or had spoken to at this point – a message.

'*I can't,*' I said. '*She might be offended because she is so much stronger than me.*'

'*If you don't ask her then you won't get your Gift back,*' they said.

Reluctant to intrude on the telephone conversation, I wrote a short note for Christine to see; *before you hang up, ask her if she has two grandmothers in the spirit world and here's the message for her if she has.*

Duly Christine checked with the medium when they'd finished.

"Mum wants to ask you a question about Spirit, is it alright?" she asked.

I almost died on the spot when my daughter said Meg was happy for me to ask her myself and she handed me the telephone to do so.

"I'm sorry," I began nervously and introduced myself. After exchanging names I said, "I have to ask – do you have a grandmother in spirit?"

"Yes," she replied.

"I don't know whether she's got white hair or grey hair, it's almost as though there are two people in one body. Would you have two grandmothers in spirit?"

"Yes, I do."

"It's just that there are two ladies here who have come to me while you were talking to Christine and they were pushing me to give you a message."

After I described them to her, I asked, "Were you closer to the white-haired lady?"

"Yes, that was my grandmother on my father's side. She was a clairvoyant and she taught me what I know to being psychic. And the grey-headed lady is my grandmother on my mother's side and *she* read tea leaves. I love them both."

I relayed their messages, which she understood and was grateful to hear and we both looked forward to meeting the following week.

After the call with the medium ended I walked back to the kitchen sink, ecstatic with the positive connection. I threw my right hand up into the air, drew a big tick and yelled, "YES!"

It was so good not only seeing the spirits, but getting a message through to another medium who I considered to be much stronger than me. I felt honoured and as I neared the sink one of the grandmothers waited to say more.

'*Now you will have to write a book,*' she said, smiling.

'*A book,*' I replied, wondering what she meant.

'*Yes, a book.*'

'*I wouldn't know what to write about!*'

'*We will help you,*' she said encouragingly.

I thought about it, still unsure what might be involved.

'*What kind of book will I write?*' I asked.

'*You are to write about all of your experiences with the spirit world,*' she instructed.

Frustrated, I replied, '*Isn't that confidential for all of the people I have read for?*'

'*Don't worry about them. As long as you don't mention names or places without their permission, you will be safe. You were given this gift,*' she went on to say, '*but you gave it back. We will guide you what to write and for each one that you remember to write about, you will receive one of your gifts back.*'

'*What will I call the book?*' I wanted to know.

"Your Encounters with the Spirit World," she answered. She even told me how to sign copies of it.

I had to think long and hard on this – I had no idea how to write a book, how or where to start with it, or whether it was going to be any good or not. Everyone fears writing 'a flop' and I didn't want to do this. I'm still learning the process, though it has helped having my daughter Christine with me in this journey. As I've written in the dedication of this book, Christine has trawled through every word of my original text, editing spelling mistakes or reconstructing grammar and sentences to make it readable.

But also, she has already gone down the publishing path and has explained to me many of the procedures that go into writing, printing and selling books. There's a lot involved, but I'm excited about it, knowing Spirit is guiding this book to wherever it may go.

When we finally met at our friend Christine's place the following week, I instantly knew which of the newcomers was the medium, for there were now three new people to our little group. I walked up to her and said, "Hi! You must be the lady I spoke to on the phone last week. My name is Joyce."

"Yes, I feel I know you from somewhere," she said with a warm smile on her face.

"Possibly it was in a past life," I said as we gave each other a hug.

By now my daughter Christine and I were getting stronger. I began to relax and she started to understand my frustrations of losing 'the gift', for she was also getting the hang of 'tuning in'. I felt I was on the spiritual road to recovery again and since going to the little group I now know just how much I really missed the spirit world's company and what comfort I have received from them.

⅏⅏

So here I am, much stronger in my psychic abilities and now able to see those in spirit with more frequency, as well as hearing them talk (not just in my mind). And this is my book – my *encounters with the Spirit World* – as presented to me by my guide or guardian angel, a kindly lady who has been a warm, loving and constant presence from the start.

The moral of this incredible journey is, if you know you have any psychic abilities, be aware that you have been given them as a *divine gift*. Don't let anyone – whether they are close to you or not – ask you to stop or to give it up, whatever their reason or reasons may be. They have no right to stand in the way of Divine Wisdom, for it is wisdom of the highest degree that has allowed you – chosen you – to have such abilities. Nothing happens by chance.

You may acknowledge them by saying "O.K.", but do NOT go through with it, only pretend to. If you really feel pressured enough it is, "o.k. to tell a little white lie," as my guides are saying to me while I write. Because you never know when you are going to need them, or maybe they [Spirit] will need your help someday.

It has been a long, hard lesson for me to get back that which I have cherished.

As I was told by Spirit, "You learned it, now you've earned it and that's all that matters. You were given this gift for a reason, now keep it!"

These days I look forward to using my gifts again – to help others that might have done what I once did, or for those in danger of losing it through fear or family pressure. I feel that if any of the readers of this book can learn from my mistake, then I will have done my job properly.

This is the lesson I had to have, no matter how hard it was for me. If I can do it, so can you.

80C3

A Meditation to Meet Someone in Spirit

For all those young and old who don't know how to meditate, or who would like to meet a passed loved one, spirit guide, guardian angel, or perhaps discover a spiritual companion, here is an exercise you may wish to follow. Make sure all telephones, radios or televisions etc. are either turned off or turned right down so as not to disturbed your session. Some people like to meditate to soft music, have incense burning, or have candles lit. Whatever your choice, ensure you are surrounded with a nice atmosphere, one that is peaceful and pleasing to your senses.

Find a comfortable chair or cushion to sit on and relax your body. If sitting on a chair, place your feet firmly on the floor and if you're seated on the floor, you may wish to try folding your legs into the lotus position. When comfortable and ready, put your hands on your knees with the palms facing upwards.

Begin by closing your eyes and imagine your body has little switches inside; in your feet, your thighs, your stomach, hands and head. Breathe slowly and easily. With your first deep breath, focus on your feet. See the switch there turning "off" as you exhale. On the second inhalation, move your focus to your lower legs and turn the switch there "off" as you breathe out. Up to your knees on the next intake and see that switch go "off" as you breathe out. Move your focus to your thighs as you inhale and switch "off" this area as you exhale. Now your legs should be feeling relaxed.

Gently take your focus to your pelvic and lower stomach region, breathing in and relaxing your muscles there. Now flick the switch "off" as you breathe out. Remind yourself that you are safe and comfortable throughout the meditation. Focus on your chest, 'see' your lungs and diaphragm fill with breath. Turn the switch "off" as you exhale, allowing this area to relax and letting go of any awareness of sounds around you.

Move your focus to your fingers. Breathe in, turn the switches "off", breathe out. See the muscles of your hands and wrists as you inhale. Switch them "off" on the out-breath. To your lower arms, breathe in and relax. Switch them "off" as you exhale. Focus on your upper arms, breathing in and relaxing. Turn the switches "off" as you breathe out. Feel your shoulders, including your collar bones as you breathe in again. Relax and switch these areas "off" as you exhale.

Now your body is relaxed and you are ready to prepare your mind for meditation. Breathe in as you focus on your neck. Relax, switching your neck "off" as you breathe out. Focus on your face as you breathe in again, relaxing your jaw, your ears, your breathing and your eyes. As you breathe out, switching "off" this region, tell yourself there are no distractions and no disharmony around you. Focus on your brain as you breathe in. Relax this area, moving your mind into a deep, sleep-like state as you switch it "off". At all times you will be aware of your surroundings without being disturbed by it. You are safe and can return to full wakefulness if you need to.

Breathe comfortably. Take a moment to enjoy being wholly relaxed, calm and untroubled by life's comings and goings. Allow yourself to feel lightweight, to feel a sense of your spiritual presence within you. This part of you is completely at peace. Your spirit-self is strong and won't let anything negative happen to you.

Now let yourself float up with your spirit-body to the ceiling and imagine you can see your earth-body below, sitting on the chair or floor. See a circle of white light surrounding this body, protecting it while you journey with your spirit. Allow yourself to float up through the roof and into the sky – higher and higher still.

You are now rising up through clouds, breathing easily, safe from gravity or falling because your spirit-self is with you.

Gradually you rise above the clouds and higher up, you begin to enter the earth's outer atmosphere, moving from blue sky to night sky, where stars shine and twinkle in space. Slowly now, look for the brightest star and when you see it, let yourself glide towards it, ever gently. It becomes brighter the closer you go, until soon you can see that it's not a star but a planet – a colourful, healthy, alive planet, with a lots of greenery on the land and blue, blue water in the seas.

It's beautiful down there and inviting. Let your thoughts be drawn into its surroundings, so that you pass gently down through its atmosphere, through clouds, down through a sunny sky, down, gently down to the land below. You come to a clean, beautiful park, lush in green grass and flowering plants, with a gently flowing river or lake to one side. Beside the waterway is a golden path, winding between flower beds and soft lawns, with sunlight falling through the tree leaves and creating flickering patches of shade beneath them.

Find a tree you like and sit beside it. Get comfortable there and for a few minutes take in the scenery; the colours, the scents, the pleasant warmth, the sounds of birdcalls and the water trickling over rocks. It is a very spiritual atmosphere, a place of infinite peace and beauty. Enjoy this lovely environment.

Presently you notice the golden path again. It attracts your eye and draws you to it. Get up and go to it in good faith it will lead you to meet someone of interest.

After the path curves around a hedge and sweeps into a small clearing, you see a person waiting for you there, smiling and welcoming your presence. Go to them, see if you recognise them. They may be someone you've known in life who has now passed into spirit, or they may be someone unfamiliar but who conveys love to you anyway.

If you don't recognise the person, ask them if they are your spirit guide, or guardian angel, or if they are someone you used to know in younger days that you may have forgotten about. Let their answer come to you in anyway it will. You may hear their name in your mind, or they may speak it aloud. Have them put across their identity in the easiest way.

When you are satisfied with their answer, acknowledge who they are, then feel free to ask them a question to a problem you may be needing a solution for. If they can, they will reply with the wisdom of spiritual understanding and insight. If you feel there is not a suitable answer, then simply enjoy their company – talk to them about whatever you wish, even if it's about unresolved issues between you both.

Listen with your heart, observe any images, colours, sounds or shapes that may accompany this person's responses, for these 'little things' help them to express the full meaning to you. It may be that your Higher Self – your spiritual intelligence – receives everything you need to know, so it is okay if you don't fully understand the actual message with your ears or eyes.

Finally, when your conversation is finished, thank them for coming to you here. Thank them for sharing their messages with you in love and open honesty. Trust this person is with you in your everyday life, even though you may not see or hear them there. Understand that whenever you want to see this person again, you need only relax, meditate on seeing a place of safety and peacefulness and they will come to you there.

When you are ready to return to your physical body, walk back down the golden path through the garden. As you return to the tree were you sat down, allow yourself to float upward into the sky. Gently rise higher and higher, up through the clouds, up to the outer atmosphere, out into the star-lit space.

Float away to where you can see our planet and draw closer to it, feeling its gentle pull bringing you back. Move steadily into earth's atmosphere and begin lowering into the sky. Down, gently down, through the cloud layers, their moisture cleansing you and helping you to feel refreshed. Don't feel hurried as you descend.

Below you can now see the land and waterways that surround the place where your body rests. Go to that place in a peaceful state; calm, unhurried and confident of your destination. Rooftops become clearer and you can see the dwelling where you need to go.

Slowly now, hover above the house where your body awaits. Be conscious of your spiritual presence – your higher self always connected to you. Let yourself be steadily lowered down through the roof, the ceiling and into the room where you can see your physical body resting.

Gently, so gently, feel yourself move into your body, entering the crown chakra of your head. Turn the switch in your brain back "on". Breathing in, turn "on" the sensory places of your face; your mouth, nose, ears and eyes. The sounds of the room can be heard quietly. Breathe out comfortably, keeping your eyes closed and relaxed until you are fully reawakened.

Focus on your neck and breathe in, switch it "on" and exhale. Move to your shoulders, breathe in, switch them "on" and breathe out. Down your arms – at your own pace – breathe in and switch them "on". Feel your wrists, hands and fingers as you breathe in again, switch them "on" and breathe out. Back up through your arms and move to your chest.

Feel your lungs and diaphragm expand as you inhale, switch these areas "on" and exhale. Lower, focus on your stomach, pelvic and buttocks areas. Breathe in, switch them "on" and breathe out. Down to your thighs, inhale, switch these upper legs "on" and exhale. Down to your knees, calves and ankles. Breathe in, switch them "on" and breathe out. Finally, feel your feet; your heels, soul and toes. Breathe in, switch them "on" and breathe out.

You can now hear the sounds of the room and you can see what is in it as you open your eyes. You are fully awake and alert and ready to return to whatever activities that may be waiting.

You can do this exercise anytime you wish; day or night, with or without company. I have had many people tell me they always feel good after this exercise, hopefully you do too.

Good Luck.

෨෬

THE END

Epilogue

If you are looking to learn more about the spirit world, may I suggest you find an open circle near you. If you can't find one, then look for a spiritualist church that could help you develop your psychic abilities. There should be one advertised in your local paper or telephone book or maybe if you have access to the internet, check this avenue out. You will be rewarded and will never look back. You be the judge – if it's what you want, good luck and Blessings!

> The Gift is a very precious thing to receive. Do not treat
> it like an old bag that you can use whenever you feel like
> it, then just throw away and expect to get it back when
> you want it to return.
> If you have learned it, then you've earned it.
> Now keep it.
> It is just like a flower – you need to nurture it.
>   J.B. Duncan.

ᘓᘒᘓ

Acknowledgements

I thank my loving husband, for without his patience I could not have written this for the spirit world as quickly as I did. He allowed me the time and space to work while being left to look after himself. He even bought me the computer I used, to write it. I would also like to thank my youngest daughter, Christine, who has given up a lot of her time in helping me with the writing and editing aspects, for which I am very grateful.

I am thankful for the teachings I received from the teachers and mediums of both the open and closed circles that I attended in the 1970's, as well as attending the Parramatta spiritualist church of New South Wales, Australia. I would like to give special acknowledgement to all of my wonderful spirit people, whom I think of as friends, for without their guidance I would not have accomplished any of my psychic work.

My beloved late father and beautiful late son both gave me their blessings for the pages that follow, and a lovely spirit lady has been with me constantly, guiding me with the retelling of my memories of these psychic experiences appearing in this book. Although I do not know her name, I believe she is one of my spirit guides. I thank them all for not having given up on me as I'd once feared they had, and for helping to teach me a very, very valuable lesson; **never** give away any special gifts that God has given you, no matter who may ask you to, or for whatever their reasons might be. At most, it is okay to **pretend** to send the spirits away, because in this sense it is alright to 'tell a little white lie' to respect those in spirit. Otherwise accept your abilities as an important part of yourself, and stand your ground in adversity.

Lastly, thank you to all the people who allowed me to use their names, and for including their stories in this book.

ഇൗരു

About The Author

J.B. Duncan was born in England in 1940 and migrated to Australia with her parents and three other siblings in 1951. As a child she didn't realise she had any 'gifts', even after seeing her first vision at the age of eleven in her new homeland. It wasn't until her later years when she developed her psychic awareness and understood what it was all about.

When she was fifteen she correctly predicted to friends that she would, "have a boy first, then a girl, another boy and, lastly a girl." She married Clive in 1961 and over the next nine years had four beautiful children; a son, Arthur, a daughter, Debbie, a second son, Kevin, and the youngest, another girl, Christine.

In her late twenties she came to terms with understanding that there was 'something different' with her emotions, and in the way she could sense seemingly impossible things happening before they came true. She yearned to know more about the spirit world and threw herself into learning everything she could about it.

She discovered there was a spiritual church in the city of Parramatta, not far from her home of the Hills district west of Sydney, and started to attend its services regularly. An open circle was held there weekly and eagerly she participated in them, gaining insight to meditation, spirit communication, even channelling. She knows that without this training she would not have been able to complete this book, for many of her abilities were developed through it.

Above all, she came to realise that spirits – our loved ones in the unseen – can help us. They never leave us despite the death of their physical bodies, because they love us.

ಬಿಂ

Printed in the USA
CPSIA information can be obtained
at www.ICGtesting.com
CBHW020306110724
11331CB00037B/257